Objects in This Mirror

OBJECTS
IN THIS MIRROR

An Anthology of Legacy

Edited by

Danielle Hanson

&

Julia Beach

Press 53

Winston-Salem

Press 53, LLC
PO Box 30314
Winston-Salem, NC 27130

First Edition

Objects in This Mirror: An Anthology of Legacy

Library of Congress Control Number
2025932278

ISBN 978-1-950413-91-1

To Mark Bilbrey and Ted Howard

and to Rick

Contents

Editors' Introduction

How do our peers shape us, as writers and as people? This anthology is both a compilation and a case study representing work from former students who shared space and time in a rare undergraduate workshop that ran continuously for forty-six years under the guidance of poet Richard (Rick) Jackson. Every year, as senior students graduated and moved into top MFA writing schools across the country, rising workshop veterans took their place as student leaders within the workshop and welcomed new students to fill empty seats and participate in this discussion-based, student driven, and often contentious workshop.

In addition to setting the reading schedule, Rick defined the rules of the workshop and set the tone every year. His style was to withhold his feedback until the end of the discussion and let students learn from each other. Poems were presented anonymously and works submitted from new students were given the same attention and sharp criticism as works submitted from seniors who had been in the workshop for years. Poems were read aloud by fellow classmates, never by the poet. Through those parameters, a culture of concentrated study and a community of writers were created. Today we ask whether those traits we learned as students can still be seen in our collective work and if they can be traced over time. What does a workshop actually do to the writers who spend time there? These are the questions this anthology seeks to examine.

Not all students in Rick's workshop continued to write, so it's important to note the participants in this collection were selected on the following criteria: they participated fully in the workshop during their tenure at the university and went on to MFA programs or continued to write and publish independently. We were students around the midpoint of this tradition. Between us, we have over forty years of editing experience, and this is easily the highest quality submission pool either of us has ever seen. Perhaps that speaks to the voice of this workshop as well—we were trained on certain poetry. We try to write poetry we would like. Perhaps there's not only a common voice to the workshop, but a common aesthetic as well. Though we find that unlikely—the participants in this book, who graduated between 1980 and 2023 have already published almost 140 books, at least ten during the production of this project. The voice and the aesthetic appear to be greater than we are.

Some moments in space/time are special, and we often don't know it until we look back. What made this workshop, taught at a public university in a blue-collar city, such a meaningful, successful training ground for poets? We think the multi-year aspect of the workshop was a significant part of it. New students progressed quickly as a direct result of hearing discussion and debate from veteran students. Although norms changed over time, for a significant period of the workshop students weren't allowed to rely on praise for their classmates' work. Rick made it clear that a workshop was not the place for praise—it was a place for work: to learn how a poem operates and to offer criticism with the same precision and interrogation an engineer would apply to building a bridge. As former student Karri (Harrison) Paul once noted in a workshop in the '90s, it was our job to note where the writer and the poem "lost and found courage."

We were made tough by the end of our studies, but it was also drilled into us that "you are not your poem." I start every workshop I teach with this lesson, and the anonymity of the poem allowed us to evaluate it for its own merits. The poem, if successful, has to make its own way in the world, away from us. This allowed us to take risks on the page. Workshops were three hours long, one evening a week. After workshop, we went down the street to eat, drink (if we were old enough), and continue the discussion until the bar closed. How many college classes extend to twice their length because students don't leave? So much instruction and knowledge was shared outside the classroom and the work didn't end there.

Students also read for national and university poetry journals, worked in translation, and interviewed writers for publications. We helped start new literary journals and managed the Meacham Writers Conference, a bi-annual writing conference that brought visiting writers to our campus each semester. Meacham attracted Pulitzer Prize winners, chancellors of the Academy of American Poets, directors of MFA programs, poets from overseas, debut authors, mid-career authors, and students. We ate potluck dinners together, discussed what we were reading, listened to each other read poetry, and shared bottles of wine. Students submitted short manuscripts and received feedback from established poets during one-on-one conferences, as well as participating in advanced workshops guided by poets we looked up to. In the tradition of doing the work we also became drivers and assistants to visiting writers, taking them to and from the airport, introducing them at readings, filling out paperwork and assisting with travel arrangements. In short, we experienced the work that went into being a writer. As participant Keith Driver noted, "Meacham was really an extension of Rick's teaching ethos—he treated us all like writers rather than writing students. Many of us came to believe that we were. Meacham was a big part of that." Many graduates of the program met their future MFA mentors at Meacham. The field was leveled and hierarchy removed. We beginners could see a writing future and understand how to get there. Many of us have returned to Meacham as visiting writers ourselves. Many of us also participated in the annual cultural summer writing trip to Slovenia, Italy, Hungary, Portugal, and other places. These trips involved art, poetry readings and conferences, meetings with local authors, writing assignments, and on-site workshops, sometimes with local poets and students. These trips were foundational to forming our view of ourselves as world citizens. We discussed literature and the history that literature draws from and resides in. We were shown the importance of translation and world poetry. We asked the question, what does it mean to write a poem that only a small population will be able to read and why does that matter. We were shown that the student has a place in the world and the world has a place in the student.

This anthology reflects a shared intense experience, but an experience that is reflected in the present. The title for this collection comes from a Richard Jackson poem, "Objects in This Mirror Are Closer Than They Appear." Our shared experience is in our rearview mirror, only seen in reflection, but the experience is within us, close, impactful. Some participants submitted work from their student days, but most submitted work from later in their writing careers. As editors, we noticed a few trends. Our poems contain a mix of history and personal, lyric/melancholic darkness, cognitive leaps, and inanimate and natural elements exhibiting human emotions and actions. We were taught that poets can (and should) lie, but emotional truth is important. This is reflected in the work in this volume, which contains many images where language and reality can't be taken at face value. Rick once told Julia a poet needs two things: imagination and glue. He said you can't buy imagination, but you can buy the glue that holds it together. The poets in this anthology never lack for imagination or glue.

The anthology is arranged by poet graduation year, so that any evolution can be tracked, and reflects:

> Decades of poetry trends, from the late 1970s to mid-2020s and how that might affect writing and subject matter

> Poets currently in their 20s to their 80s and how that might affect writing and subject matter

> Poets just beginning their writing careers and very established writers

We knew we were somewhere special. Not because we were somewhere elite, but because we were surrounded by a passion for the same thing. We were vested in our work and each other. Our professors took us seriously, not just Rick, but the larger community as well. Visiting writers took us seriously. So we took ourselves and our classmates seriously. As several participants noted, "workshop was family." Many participants said that workshop changed the trajectory of their life. You don't have to be perfect to have impact, but you have to be invested, and Rick was invested in each of us, in our writing and in us as people. And we were and are invested in each other.

For our entire lives, UTC's workshops have been the foundation of how to write and what to write. One poet mentioned that she selected a poem to submit because it had been chosen for a nationally renowned journal and therefore a poem whose quality she was confident about. What she probably didn't know was that the editor of that journal is a UTC graduate, and that editor didn't know the poet was a UTC graduate either. This anthology is meant to be a reflection on a community voice, and how a workshop can influence and develop writers, and whether you can see that mutual influence on writers' work even decades later. We think the answer to this is a resounding yes. This anthology was never meant to be a tribute, but it is. It never could not be. So to Rick, thanks. And to all of you who were in the classroom, thanks. It is an honor to be a part of this community and legacy. I hope you each enjoy this as much as we do.

—Danielle Hanson and Julia Beach

By the Numbers

Workshop participants have:

Written/edited 140 books, including ten-plus new books since we started the project. Forty percent of participants have published books.

Received awards and honors including MacArthur Scholar, Fulbright Scholar, Stegner Fellow, NEA Grant Recipient, Geisel Award, Golden Kite Award for Picture Books, Sydney Taylor Book Award for Younger Readers, Guggenheim Award, Pushcart Prize, PEN Award for Literary Translation.

Worked on editorial staffs for over twenty-five journals and presses: *Black Warrior Review, Lyric Poetry Review, Crab Orchard Review, Gulf Coast, Indiana Review, Pebble Lake Review, Poetry Miscellany, The Porch, Josephine Quarterly, Hayden's Ferry Review, Iowa Review, North American Review, The Massachusetts Review, Michigan Quarterly, B O D Y, Arts and Letters, Minyan Magazine, Atlanta Review, Kirkus Review, Loose Change Magazine, Carriage House Review, Killing the Buddha,* Slapering Hol Press, Doubleback Books, Sundress Publications, *Narrative Collective.*

Translated work from Czech, Slovene, Arabic, German, and Spanish.

Received MFA/PhDs at twenty-four institutions, including ten graduates of the Iowa Writers Workshop; four each from University of Houston and Indiana University; three each from the University of Maryland College Park, Southern Illinois University at Carbondale, and Vermont College; and two each from UNC Greensboro, Arizona State University, UNC Wilmington, Western Michigan University, University of Massachusetts Amherst, University of Alabama, and Georgia State University; and one each from Johns Hopkins

Writing Seminars, Syracuse University, University of Washington, Virginia Tech, Georgia College & State University, University of Tennessee Knoxville, University of Denver, Eastern Tennessee State University, University of Tennessee Chattanooga, Sewanee University, Duke University, and University of Utah.

Worked at the Poetry Society of Tennessee, Sundance Institute, Library Foundation of LA, USC Online.

Taught at over thirty-eight colleges and universities: University of Michigan, Indiana University, University of California, Irvine, California State University-Northridge, Miami University (Ohio), Boise State University, University of Utah, University of Tennessee Chattanooga, Emory University, Eastern Tennessee State University, Hamline MFA Program, University of Denver, University of Texas, Kennesaw State University, Otis College, St. Olaf College, Johns Hopkins University, Owens Community College, Heartland Community College, Teikyo Westmar University, University of Iowa, Maryland Institute College of Art (MICA), Towson University, University of Alabama, University of Northern Iowa, Georgia College & State University, University of West Georgia, Southern Illinois University, Arizona State University, University of Houston, Furman University, Western Illinois University, University of Virginia Arlington, Tennessee Christian University, Robert Morris College, Lee University, Cleveland State University, Chattanooga State Community College, and Covenant College.

Taught in high schools and jail programs, including Turn the Page and Girls Correctional Institute.

Worked together at journals and presses, won the same publication prizes, attended graduate school together (including four to six simultaneously at Iowa and three simultaneously at Indiana), married each other, edited projects together (including this one), became pressmates, been high school friends, lived together, been siblings, met for online workshops, reviewed each other's books, taught each other in high school.

Several former students (at least twenty to thirty) of contributors have also published books. Many of us would say our teaching style is heavily influenced by our undergraduate experience.

Thank you

For my student at her first open-mic night

for reading
your ass-kicking poem
and thank you trusting
it to our hearts and pencils
and thank you once again
for accepting my editions
which were offered
only because you are good
enough at the craft of building
up a poem line by line
from dirt and daub
that I believe you
felt the same breeze
I did when it slipped
damply through the gaps.

Richard Seehuus

Rachel Landrum Crumble

Again

We parted, stoic characters in a 1940's wartime movie—
Grief, waving a white hanky on the pier.
It took hours in the blinding heat
for the steamer to finally pull away.

I, a helpless spectator on deck,
counted hankies until I was dizzy.
Who doesn't suffer loss?

Eventually, I saw the world—the Alps,
Venice, the Pyramids. That long ago farewell
no more than a dark line on the sea's horizon.

Months into the journey,
on a flawless blue day
I spotted Grief waiting at the pier
in a gray fedora and trench coat
as we neared a foreign port of call—Malta, or Haifa.
Something not unlike love
leapt in my heart.

I thought "good-byes" your forte,
didn't expect to meet again
so far from where I started
on an ordinary lovely day.

Courage for a New Year

All familiar things
are released of connotation.
In these early hours, starting over
seems possible:

A shoe on the step
becomes hopeful, loses
its dereliction—
was going somewhere
all along.

Paper clutter
on a bedroom shelf
vibrates with history.

Old photos, proof
of a hard-won past
forecast an unexpected
cheery present.

The blank page is a blizzard,
and on dogsled we course our way
through blinding brightness.

While the year is young,
it seems possible to arrive.
We cannot lose our way
before we find it.

Liz Albert

Storm at Evening

When I raise the shade on the storm settling
at the edge of town, I think of rain

drumming the roof of my mother's house
when the kitchen windows cloud with steam

from macaroni boiling on the stove.
My sister and I, busy at homework,

squint in the light from some old re-run
making neat columns of numbers, rows of c's and d's—

the clatter of spatulas and spoons,
the rattle of papers, canned laughter, and the low,

steady rain. Her lips in a soft "o,"
Mother blows the foam in the pot

back to nothing and watches it build again
like her desires, indistinct, suspended

for the moment in the sounds of the house,
the heat, what there is. At the edge of town,

the pink strip of sunset thins, winks out.
The clouds flatten to a sheet of rain,

and I think of my mother, alone in her house,
how she stands at the stove, first

stirring her pot of soup,
then warming her hands in the steam.

Nothing You Can See

It isn't anything you can see.
Sometimes, during droughts, the swamp
burns, trapping the white-tailed deer
who can't outrun the flames.
It's only the smell of smoldering heat
That reaches us here. When I was a child
I thought it was the end of the world.

The azalea bushes we brought home in tin cans
have grown taller than the porch now,
and you sleep with a man who is not my father.
The familiar crack of wood floors
as they cool in the night air,
the gentle whir of the ceiling fan,
can't ease the words that tighten in my throat
as I watch heat lightning
through your window screens.

For years I've tried to forget
the things that are trapped in those hollow sounds.
The scratchy wool suit I cried into
the day father left, the closet light
that burned all that night, my own voice
calling to no one in a dream.

David Breitkopf

The Final Song of the Musicians

When we come to this secluded lake
You will find the ground soft and fertile.
In the eastern corner I'll show you the grave
Sites—the tombstones straight as teeth
Around the water's lip, forming a mouth. But no song
Can be heard from the musicians

Buried there. As the story goes five musicians
Drowned mysteriously one night on a boat on the lake.
Their instruments are interred along with their final song
At the lake's bottom, which is why they say the soil is so fertile.
Sometimes people leave things of themselves here, even teeth
As good luck. How odd to find a tooth on top of a grave.

I don't mean to scare you with all this talk of graves.
But I'm always hoping to hear the final song of the musicians
When I come here. At night when it gets cold and my teeth
Chatter, I often stand at the edge of the lake
Listening. The stars seem to give off a fertile
Light, and it reminds me of a mournful song,

A chantey, that an ex-lover of mine sang
At the site of her mother's grave.
It was just her voice and the fertile
Wind carrying her words like seeds. She needed no musicians
To back her. I took her to this very lake
Once. It was she who found the tooth

On the grave. She compared it to her own teeth,
Which were charmingly crooked. And when she sang
To me one night out here near the soughing lake
Sitting in front of these humble graves
I swear I could hear those musicians
Humming along. But perhaps that's just my fertile

Imagination. I tell you this because our love is more fertile
Then ever. There's a strength in it like teeth.
And though I'd never call us great musicians,
There is a true harmony in the song
We sing to each other. Our voices are even engraved
On the stones we will be buried beneath at the bank of this lake.

So let us now enter the lake up to our teeth
And beyond until our own fertile song
Can be heard by those noble and grave musicians.

Piano

For Aunt Jeanette

Passing, mid-chore, through the living,
I disturb the piano's sepulcher
with a flat, minor-chord misgiving—
hammer to an inaudible rupture

of the current, which courses the porous vase
set atop my mother's upright.
Out of discord, stirs a counter-trace—
sonata ashes sifting in moonlight

strain through the permeable mystery,
as though an expiring breath of air
could wind its way home from history.
Sacred zephyr, sweep aside the folds of my ear,

linger, bearer, within the leitmotif,
to sculpt in sound—your face in bas-relief.

David Franke

One True Thing

Daniel washes Dorothy's hair
in the kitchen, at the sink, one
late morning in May
because she's afraid
to let some young woman
press her frail spine against the cold
porcelain and quiz her about TV
and the grandkids and lie about how thick
her hair has become. Our mother, a small-town
beauty queen, bent now, unspools
stories as Daniel first wets her hair,
wipes water from her eyebrows.
She is talking the way a fly knocks against a window
because she has been injured somehow
by being alone with her thinking,
so her son, who rubs shampoo
between his hands to warm it,
gently, like smoothing a child's scarf,
eases the lather below our mother's ears to the nape
of her neck. His nails are chipped and blued
from errant hammerstrikes.
You could peel a raw egg without spilling it,
Dorothy says, and Daniel rinses her hair by scooping
warm water in his palm and directing it
over her scalp. She talks about doctors,
she says *You are my man now* and *Some days
I just want to die.* He raises her up
wordlessly, tucks a towel around her narrow shoulders,
and she looks up at him from the chair with wonder,
as if she just remembered the one true thing.

AM Radio

September erodes an entirely new shoreline out of morning. Like
last night in the car, coming home in a puzzled dark. I mean, mist
standing in patches over the road, haunting it. I am trying to say
driving home, the marriage over, the kid's beds taken down, their
rooms repainted, ready for some other family—fumbling at the
radio lands me in AM. Who unlocks what cinder-block station in
some cornfield to pour words down a mike that drains to the sky?
Their only audience is guys like me. Once I drove to the only high
point in our county to get AM and smoke pot, listening to the signal
twitch off the stratosphere in a dark Iowa night, late like this, all
for a little Jethro Tull. My headlights dim in the mist and rebound;
I get each station for five seconds, I get voices on voices, consonants
and static, notes and knobby arguments struggling. Ending is like
this, I think, vowels and images blindly tearing past each other. Then
it rests, warbling between two stations from another time zone.
AM is the sound of all our pasts playing at the same time. Noise
bristles like nettles that numb my knuckles for days. The music of
sleeplessness, shopping carts, internal combustion engines. If we love
people because they show us who we are, who are we when they are
gone? I can taste copper in the AM radiation, signal fraying like the
cheap rope I used for hauling my children's furniture home on the
roof of my car a long time ago. I mean, in a September like this one,
but not as strange, a commonplace day with miles ahead, the radio
guitar pulled taut and then some, sustained and clear, stretching and
weightless and rising.

Jami Loree

Some Regrets of My Own

For L.O.

I. Knowledge
It is this way:
you and I once shared cider
and conjugated French verbs.
My lost watch ticked on
another woman's arm. Your wife
listened from the kitchen.

From October to March, I wrapped myself
in down, covered my head
with wool, my hands with fleece,
and let the wind drive me. You knew
I was there.

II. Desire
You kept turning up
when I'd counted on being alone.
The soccer field, the bus,
three beers into a harp and dulcimer.

The rain came again. Blackberry
brambles squeezed up between concrete
and pavement. We picked
our hands and mouths full
from the side of a downtown street.
Night, the Pink Elephant Car Wash sign
blinked on and off, pink light pulsing
my room: pink bookcase, table, bed, you
in the only chair, light
then dark again.

III. Silence
For instance, we spoke of God
but never prayed.
Summer in Seattle and everyone
forgets. (Winter
covers its suicides, hides the mountain
we think isn't there.) I went south
anyway. Humid nights
my sheets clung to me; mine
the only car on the causeway at sunrise.
Flash of new sun off the waves
was a code, someone in distress
signaling over and over for help.

The Year in Tampa

I remember windless afternoons
drinking wine from coffee mugs,
we'd watch for alligators in the lake,
the eye and nostril that barely broke
the surface, the monster shadow
of the body beneath.
We played backgammon in bed
every night. Fat beetles smacked
the lighted window like popcorn.
We fried pork chops, ate them
with applesauce and canned corn.
Nights out, we swallowed raw
oysters with Saltines and beer.
More than once, we both fell
asleep on the long drive back from town,
the car muttering into a ditch.
And I remember how, making the bus trip
back from the beach, you stood
over a little boy riding alone,
and when he fell asleep, leaned over
and took the bobbing head in your hand,
carefully held it all the way to St. Pete.

1969

These fingers flamed red in the snow when I was ten:
Numb at first, then pricklish, then the cold pain set in.
These fingers felt the first buds, and carried the stink of dogwood
          bark into the kitchen;
They felt the heart battering in the bird's hot pocket and their own
          pulse pressed to its throat.

These fingers—nineteen sixty-nine—feel the warm sheets
Where grownups have passed the night,
The pig's dimpled neck, the wings in the web of the black widow,
And the cat's tongue rasp of mint leaves in the mildewed shadows
Where the water pipe drips.

Everywhere these fingers. In the brittle downswung hair
          of a woman,
In shadows spat on brickwalls, in rushing water,
In the little maps blue and red on the sleeping man's eyelids.

Greedy under the deaf-mute moon,
Under the shrubs where cats are munching lizards;
Sweat-slick in hurry and fear, in the closets of chalk-dust
          and soft depression;

They are everywhere.

They are quiet now these fingers, folded palm to palm;
The thumbs dropped, cocked a little, like anchors;
(the boy asleep now, the blue light on);
The four fingers tucked, almost distinguishable;
Like the three shapes the king called to in the fire—
Shadrach, Meshach, Abednago—
And the fourth shape that the king could not name.

Paul Said This

If I were a ranch I'd be the Bar None.
—Rita Hayworth in *Gilda*

Mozart was part dog, part genius, his hot flame
Aloyius craved a Prince, instead, and bucked him downstairs
To Constanze, her sister, who was a dog too—so goes the story—
Paul is on his third Whitbread Stout, expansive but unaware
Of my 7 AM appointment at the airport, our voices
Lap a dog-like flop in the eyes of the waitress whose belief

In our sobriety (or is it propinquity?) is waning, like all good belief
Tends to do anytime, anywhere—rain-snow-or-sleet. The flame
That socks sadness into Mozart's songs is that the voice
And piano never touch, i.e. consummate (says Paul). So M. was
        upstairs—
Minded composing his lieder, thinking of long-gone Aloyius,
        and unaware
Of body/soul, light/dark, the twain shall never etc. This story's

One more offshoot to a whole other story,
And like history boils down to a problem of belief,
Both in and of the narrator, the talker, in this case Paul, unaware
Of my right-now-scritching pencil. He was on Blood Mountain,
        agog at a flaming
Dusk and the "ground stars" (house lights) below like the staring
Eyes of every life passed on and trussed up under the earth.
        One voice,

Soprano, soared out the convertible of a man who taught voice
At a girls' school and who was so ugly Paul's dog Sue (another story)
Would not take a sandwich from him, but thrashed the stair—
Steep banks of Mountain Laurel, which is sort of like Bay Leaf,
Only poisonous (Ask your forest ranger!). Paul was with <u>his</u> flame,
Less hot, an interior decorator, abused by her father but unaware

Of this as abuse, and (moonlighting) a caterer too, unaware
Her mushrooms "a la Greche" and raw pea pods voiced
In a starburst pattern (the tart tepid flame
of a curry dip stoking up the center!) was her very best story
On how her daddy hurt her. What's debilitating in belief's
How belief's disguised, shifting, day to day, according to every
morning at the stairs

What's waiting? Paul never could crack his lover's Mona Lisa stare.
(This too's important, a further story of which you'll remain
        less than aware)
Even when the ugly teacher's Mozart pierced the horizon. Paul
        doesn't forget. Belief
Binds all the separate strangling strands into a single voice.
Mozart somehow hatches sadness and joy at once. A "story"
When I was a boy meant a lie, and you held onto that lie like a
candle-flame

Taken tip-toe up the stairs. Tell me, is this dawn's shivering
        peach flame
Certain, uncertain? Voice or echo? You go to bed believing
        a story you know
Is just a story. You like that. History makes us all dogs (let them
        lie!): bone-fed, barking, unaware.

Laurie Perry Vaughen

Train Diorama

My son leans into the glass to watch for the train.
He trusts this world.
His arms trail behind him like a line of Lionel.
Unlike him, I find this milltown mural
unlike the word *hometown*.
But my son is four, and looks up to a world
of mountains, trestles, and men.
Here, there are no power-poles, sewer drains, subdivisions.
The journey is all
sticky smear and mystery tunnels.
He's ready with an engineer's bandana
to swipe away at grime and grit, and he'll have both.
I watch him emerge with the train. He's driving now.
He's turning a curve. *Look. Look.* A neighbor. An apple tree.
A tire swing. A town. His voice is all whistle—
never wooden or souvenir. I see his reflection
in the bakery, the library, this world lined up
like sturdy books, spines of 19th century buildings.
Here, street lights flame mid-day, a candy-cane
barbershop spins men into gray.
There's no building marked VA. The orchard
long ago became graves, but here, the teacher apples
get the best slope, and the grower, with his basket
of unbruised Red Delicious, waves at each train,
waves us on, to plod the carpet path around the town
that is worn, *threadbare*. We pace, endangered
as red wolves, the ones in rehab at the zoo,
pacing a place made for our own good. For now,
I do not break into the boy's dream, hesitate to trespass
in the scene where a boy waves at a string that seems
to connect all things into an infinity of old ideas
that the car loaded with coal is innocent as the hay.

Touring Elizabeth Bishop's Nova Scotia

A poet drifts by with a net.
Her books swell, accordions
of labored breath.

A fence of oars blooms
and we begin to see everything
as budding, a refiguring.

Her words find us:
fish, map, house, bus, church.
Her words find us standing in rain,
drenched in splintering dreams.

Her words find us waiting:
like children eager for their orange
slice of a bus, a fog of wild animals,
for the red house to crow,
for the cold iron stove to settle, root
into its plank floor,

for the white cradle
of a rig we rent
to buoy us through her blue rocks,
as our ordinary motor hums a hymn
of *fish, map, house, bus, church.*

Khaled Mattawa

Double Portrait with Trains

The morning a promise
neither false nor true.
She makes coffee, the taste
of cardamom and a sweetness
she cannot recall.
Mabruka served us
cookies and light tea
in porcelain cups,
the handles shaped like fish.
This from a social call
twenty-four years ago.
We gave their baby a bracelet
with a big Allah engraved
next to his name.
"The baby" operating a train
between Aswan and Asyut
as we speak. I listen.
Her laughter, and the past
a spool of tales
unwinding. An hour.
Now I must leave.
She is happy
I have work to do.

*

A train whistle
and I cling to handlebars
as though it were my last chance
at birth. In the cabin
my thoughts stutter
no further than the window,
never penetrating the glass.
Why did I go see her village?
Buffalo carcasses

floating on channels
and channels suffocating
with water hyacinths.
Pot-bellied grain boats stranded
and a boy sleeping on deck,
flies swarm his thin face.
She lived beside the train tracks.
She lived and played
and waited for the caboose
to shake her home.
And the musty smell of the cow stall
and the mule, a depository
of rage and affection,
a whole family of angry kicks,
and the boy called
to piss on its wound.
They waited for the train,
for the day to slip like a shovel
in the metallic taste of dirt.
Weddings and feasts—
oboes and clarinets drift
to nearby villages beckoning
guests and pariah dogs.
And the meals of lentils and rice,
the head of a calf
hung above the day,
a charm, and proof
nothing was spared.
But who ate its heart and tongue?
No one knows.

*

We are not in a valley.
Cow bells in the afternoon.

We are not looking at a river.
Fishing boats, miles of nets.
We are in a London mall.
"Like a mouse
in the Pasha's storeroom,"
she is astounded by the choices,
filling bags with dresses
and cheap shoes.
Her neighbors
Her extending tribe.
Then she sees the toddler,
blue eyes, blonde curls, picks it up,
a flurry of kisses and hugs,
and God bless and God protect,
the father—enraged—
rushing toward her pulling
the baby from her embrace—
his face a universal sign of disgust.
On the train,
her bags at her feet,
she is dejected and wants
to go home. She turns to me.
But I have no pity to give.

*

The road a ribbon
paralleling the railway,
stitches on the desert floor.
She rides west now
and now is then.
Before the cramped resorts.
Before the road swelled,
shoulders pockmarked
by watermelon stalls.

And confetti.
Millions of black plastic bags.
Hollow crows.
No, no, I was not the child
who wept, *Let us go back,*
the one who was laughed at
for years. She rides west now
in a van, two daughters
at her side. They see the train
and drive beside it for hours.
And for hours the children wave
at strangers and strangers
wave back at them.
After Marsa Matrouh
they crane their necks
searching for it
until someone remembers
that at Marsa Matrouh
the railway ends.

Ecclesiastes

The trick is that you're willing to help them.
The rule is to sound like you're doing them a favor.

The rule is to create a commission system.
The trick is to get their number.

The trick is to make it personal:
No one in the world suffers like you.

The trick is that you're providing a service.
The rule is to keep the conversation going.

The rule is their parents were foolish,
their children are greedy or insane.

The rule is to make them feel they've come too late.
The trick is that you're willing to make exceptions.

The rule is to assume their parents abused them.
The trick is to sound like the one teacher they loved.

And when they say "too much,"
give them a plan.

And when they say "anger" or "rage" or "love,"
say "give me an example."

The rule is everyone is a gypsy now.
Everyone is searching for his tribe.

The rule is you don't care if they ever find it.
The trick is that they feel they can.

Beatitudes

1.
My child wants to know if the mountains really cowered.
"How do you know when a sea or a river is afraid?
How do you know when the sky is thinking yes or no?

And why did Adam say yes—Did he know that
all the other creatures refused? Was he arrogant
or just ignorant? Was he God's last choice?"

2.
"Did you really have a party the day the dictator died?
And you had a cake decorated with all the flags?
Did you think his death will fix everything?

Why did we spend all that time there?
Why couldn't we just stay here?
Isn't this our country too?

And all these people fleeing and drowning,
what are they hoping for? Whose fault is it?
How long must we wait for things to improve?"

3.
She speaks to me in our language
in front of her friends, to share a secret,
or—cool and beaming—to show off.

I wonder how long it will last, this pride,
this intimacy. Sometimes she puts her arm
next to mine and tells me I have the lighter skin.

"Why are you doing this," I ask.
But she doesn't point to the flag
or say, "It's the way of the world."

Instead she tells me not to worry, that she is "the most
kid kid in my class, the least mature one, Baba!"
Not all kinds of wisdom console, I tell her.

Then I begin to think of words she'll soon hear
that can make her wish she wasn't who she is.
Lead me to virtue, O love, through the smoke of despair.

4.
"Let's walk through the woods," she tells me.
"Let's walk by the rocky shore at sunrise."
"Let's walk through the clover fields at noon."

In the rainforest she is silent, mesmerized.
She'd never prayed—we never taught her—
but she seemed to then, eyes alert with joy.

She points to a chameleon the size of a beetle,
teaches me the names of flowers and trees,
insects we can eat if we're ever lost here.

"I'm teaching you how to entrust the world
to me," she says. "You don't have to live
forever to shield me from it."

Shannon Smith-Lee

Sears Wish Book, 1980

There was a flaw in him that urged him to catalogue
rather than enjoy.
        —J.M. Ledgard

The best parts left everything to wish for—
shirtless, tawny men on treadmills
early in the days of laying things bare.

Christmas came hard and early that year.
I stayed in my room shopping for thrills.
The best parts left everything to wish for,

studs in bathing suits and tented underwear
arranged like electric candles on sills,
early in the days of laying things bare.

I could "read" it, innocent, in an armchair,
browsing home gyms and honing my skills.
The best parts left nothing to wish for,

hard men in bathrobes with sharp blond hair,
capable and broad, in control of their wills.
It was early in the days of laying things bare.

I know what I did to her wasn't fair—
marrying, fathering, ignoring how I feel.
The worst parts have nothing left to wish for,
now, when everything has been laid bare.

The Underhouse

When it hasn't rained for a week,
the hummock in the middle of our yard
splits like a sausage on the grill,
and you see black hollows underneath.
When the August sun is all but gone,
you hear faint voices seeping out.

When we dug up the sewer line to fix it,
we saw the bricks of an old cistern
like another house underground.
Years later, there are faint dips in the yard,
an occasional hole emerging overnight
which must be filled in and leveled flat.

This must be the work of those inhabitants
of the under-house, striving for contact.
Their lines are down. They're afraid for us.
They need to know we are alive and well,
up here in all that light, all that air.
They send us earnest prayers of help,

alone as we are with the roving beasts,
the biting flies. In the dark after the moon
is quenched, I walk the hill to the back gate,
and on the rarest of occasions, a hand
reaches from the earth and grabs my foot,
not as if to kill, not as if to hurt, just

a hand holding for the barest moment,
not wanting to let me go, out of love.

Richard Seehuus

Options

You aren't complete, you are completely
In thrall, a chipmunk locked
On the grassless path at risk
For getting noticed or not noticed

Doing nothing is worse
Than doing the wrong thing
You are a pencil unsharpened
You are a pocketknife unopened

We are, none of us, whole
But holding only what we have
Is holding smoke, is missed
Exits, is a thousand destinations
Which is nowhere, is neither coast
Nor woods, anywhere is equidistant
From where you stand inside your trembling
Body hearing footfalls pass you by

Little Bear

Little bear
Upright, awakened
Rudely by the hikers' bell
Less a warning than a call
To enter the ring

Catherine Wagner

From "The City Has Sex with Everything"

The city has sex with Megan

  when the air shaped like the inverse of Megan
accepts Megan as she moves.

    If Megan is a system of exchange
that floats her labor and her point

    of view in vapor/liquid soup
  passàging through her valves

and if her later corpse, collapsing,
  updates its inversion of the air

  even more than did the air displace
when she grew from brown-eyed baby

into strong laboring woman in blue jeans
    and heathered wool,

and if the air and earth draw from Megan's corpse
  all the energy and minerals

  she pulled from her surrounds
  to build her nails and bones and teeth—

  if the exchange doesn't stop
but only ceases to support her consciousness,

  and if her consciousness was corpse anyway until
it found relation,

  then what demises
is the potential for the human social,

and another sociality
will unbutton my whole shoe

and tongue hang limp,
what sex is for but stops me

at the barrier, a pixelated
glamor reef though very

close and simple, smell a
flurry, parapluie paraphrase,

energy funneled through a shape.
You filtered chemical

information in such a pointy
fulgent scrambled way, in the city

and outside the city in the vernal zones
and aqua zones the city shaped, flow-charted, realist

trucked. The city caved under
when the zones rose and lapped around the pilings,

manged foundations green,
rotted the teeth out of the mouth of the city,

harbor high-rises
dark and blown. The city is extremely fragile tender

human mesh and will be mush
and mushrooms grow in, there is room in, ruins

roam the rearticulated harm.

From "Of Course"

An I was built to rip a
we apart?

Create
remonstrable success. Remonstrable outcomes.

Laptop sticker: "Kill your local rapist" well he's
so likely to be your dad tho.
Kill him.

....

In my mother's belly I'm a tramp
And her heartbeat presages my orgasm, judders my whole blood.
As awkward combinations unionize.
So please pursue discomfort across skin.

....

What nucleates sky ice
for cloud formation?
Plankton poop,
dirt-sized, caught up in mist.

Build heaven of excrement
That engines [v.] rain [n.].

Used

Dressed to strangle, like Frankenstein's monster:
my new second-hand skin donated
by the fashionable or the dead, their closets
sorted through by daughters and neighbors—
I could be ready to go anywhere

in this satiny, slightly pilled scarlet sweater,
in the skirt a size small but the perfect hue,
tight in that starlet way across the hips—don't look
too close and it's glamorous—these shoes
already slant-worn at the heels, tipping my gait unsteady.

I could've been ready to see you, with your—yes—
salesman's smile and doe-eyes, your mime's hands insisting
a world one almost believes is there,
your mechanic's hands failing at reconstruction,
that pull and pick at your shirt patched

on the heartside with someone else's name.
I am a miserable seamstress, too impatient—
my alterations always look like compromise, uneasy
truce drawn between me and my materials. You
had that half-sewn look, you *seemed* too much—

And I, shear-tongued, needle-eyed:
don't be fooled. I'm not got up as smart
as I think. Tonight, shepherding someone else's house
and pets, I'm the little girl in the corner, quiet,
moving letters around a puzzle: *hope—open,*

heart—tart—art—useless to redress harm.
Or maybe not. Say it: these thrift-shop clothes
crease with my body like my own skin.
You're back with her. I have here your efficient,
dishwasher's hands, guiltless, bleached

exceptionally clean, your eyes-in-absentia,
little targets—. Anger is too much work.
On someone else's TV, I watch Koko,
the signing gorilla, name a tailless kitten "All-Ball,"
scoop the splay-footed mewing thing

onto her chest, gentle-handed. Someone else's dog
lays his head on my leg. Can it hurt to love
someone else's dog? It's when All-Ball dies
and Koko signs "frown-sad-cry"
that I weep, safe in a room where nothing is mine.

Portrait of Childhood with Abstract Art

The child was raised by Malevich canvases—*Black Square, White on White*—in a simple geometry of feeling. What could be more helpful than billboards, icons, flat planes uncluttered with the treacherous figuration of words? The child looked up into glowering Black Square, studied the off-white of White on White for hours, wondering what was its secret, its cool, angular serenity undisturbed by Black Square's sharp contrast & violent edges. The child looked back & forth, making, as children do, the inscrutable tell it a story with its silence, its all-&-nothing. It watched Black Square drinking, like gravity, from the well of White on White, all light & color sucked into its sharp-cornered heart. Together an ourobouros, Moebius strip, finite to finite bonded, making infinity. The child began to wonder where it had come from; it could not have come from or between them.

Outside, the wind shook dry leaves left on trees, stormclouds glowered dull metal above. Or light whitened the windowglass hot to touch. The child believed that it came from the air, full of sky & rain, & from the light, which disappeared but always returned, & from the keening sound the wind made against the sharp-cornered house. The child believed the voices that sliced out of far rooms sometimes harshly & the ones that brushed its ear like a wing. From them, it learned that fathers are towers, stonehard & lordly, mothers righteous & still, a placid lake that mirrors the sky. Sometimes, father & mother would take human form. Sometimes a nosy dog would greet the child delightedly & a squirrel would teach the child how food could be buried & found again. The child came to believe that it was not an orphan but the opposite—born to everything, child of everything, at home everywhere—for which there is no single word, *orphan's* antonym, but each day a new one. Today, *weathervane*, yesterday, *peregrine*, tomorrow, *howl*.

Paper Anniversary

For Anu

How do we include the world? How to bring
everything to witness? To invite the air, the light,
the waters and mountains, the soil and
growing things, the gods and all of time? How
to bring everything we love to witness love?
The coolest day of a long, hot summer and the sun
shone in patches through the leaves,
through the clouds. Our families gathered,
and blessed us. Flowers shone their bright faces and
the smell of sunshine on the grass. Ladies in
bright saris made their way to folding chairs
and the murmur of their smiles as they blessed us.
Kids spun through the dance floor
like gusts of wind and musicians
tuned their strings. And we arrived,
as we always arrive in our own lives,
with smiles and laughter and a
touch of surprise—a horse,
a tuxedo, a glittering waterfall of
a dress, a love song. We arrived
with love. We blessed each
other with love. We blessed
everyone. And the sun came out
golden and blessed us. Shadows
dappled by the hands of leaves
blessed us. Clouds the great temples
in the sky held their holy space aloft
for us. Grasses hushed close
and the flowers turned their faces to us.
Fire crackled fed and danced
for us. Children played and gave
their laughter for us. Farmers and
cooks together made meals for us.
Musicians played sang and stomped

for us and everyone danced.
Everyone ate and fed each other.
Everyone laughed and sang and
played and clapped and raised a glass.
Everyone smiled and swayed
and held each other and raised
their hands and touched each other
and placed their hands on us
and together with the flowers
and the grasses and the clouds
and the leaves and the sun
and the bold open sky they blessed us.
They blessed each other.
And it may have rained just a
sprinkle for luck And someone may
have got a little too drunk
with love And shoes lay forgotten
by the dance floor And the cake was all gone
but not the sweetness And the fireflies
joined the cousins and the crickets
in their conversations And the dance-off
ended in a draw.
But before the last love song
rang out toward the lake
Before they picked across
the wet grass to their cars
Before the last cider was tipped
and the goodnight hugs
You and I had already
slipped away to a quiet place
Leaving this evening as a gift,
a memory, a moment we could all carry,
a moment that would carry us
into the next year.

Father's Day

His fingers cling to mine as the nurse
threads new needles into his veins.
He shivers with the effort of breath,
the weight of the day. I hold him
steady, my attention still
with the passivity of just waiting
for fresh antibiotics to kick in.

Tomorrow in the sunshine he will
climb back to us, shaken and pale
as a newborn, eyes wide taking in light.
Tomorrow will be Father's Day.

But tonight, as now, he will float naked
and shivering in amniotic night, adrift
above the ocean of dark and stars
beyond counting reflected in his face.
This face, so like my own, both unafraid
and unawake to the long evening,
let's bring on the morning together,
one hand holding the other as we face the light.

Helga Kidder

At St. Mary's Convent, Sewanee, TN

Wouldn't it be easy to die here
my friend says, looking
on forests of aspen and oak
fall brushes with golden haloes.
Charcoal clouds striate the sky
as wind pinches leaves to let go.

Wonder who named the roads
we've left behind,
Rattlesnake Springs Lane,
Rule of St. Benedict Circle,
Angels' Rest.

Here we learn how to grow
edible landscaping: Plant Jerusalem
artichoke next to marigold,
nasturtium between squash,
allium among Red Russian kale.

Ora et labora—the nuns believe
in prayer and work. Hands seeding dirt,
seeds lifted to heaven
as leafy plants, flowers, all edible
kinds of prayer.

A nun, bent over the bar
of a walker strolls her tabby,
perched on the seat like a lady in waiting,
through the hall leading to the door,
showing us the way.

Luna Moth

When I saw you again, homeless,
blending into the light-grey of the house,
your viridescent wings held flat against
the siding, I spoke to you with tenderness
as if I saw an old friend after two years.
You did not move, just took in my words,
your painted eyes cast down, already losing
perspective in your one-day world.
Are you an omen? A portend to hold on?
You've come so far to press your tiny soul
against the house, grasping what I as well
cling to in storms that lash and rasp nagging
the walls, our breaths leaving tiny trails
that still hinge us to life.

Danielle Hanson

Domestic Troubles

The cloud awoke this morning,
ashamed, knelt at the back door,
begging forgiveness. The wind was
hiding under a teacup—such
havoc when uncovered: papers
blown across the floor, pets blown
into corners. Sometimes our ties
are our undoing—can nothing
in this world be trusted?
The tender morning pulls leaves
over head, trembling.

Night's View of Fog

I planted the seeds of dew
and one grew,
lifting into sky.
I climb it high
to a platform on which
to reach stars as
my beanstalk dissolves
into day. The air
holds its breath
until I fall, hard
and complete.

Ted E Howard

Mural from a Small Church in the Slovene Countryside

Dressed from peasant to priest they dance
from left to right holding hands.
Not the way I would imagine dancing
into the grave. Not that I would really know
what to think or how to dress or if it really matters
what doom looks like. But the idea
that someone might lead me happily
into that moist cellar of earth
to lie in the scent of stale roots.
That I would go without thinking twice
about a summer cloud passing over.
That I would go without even glancing back
at the smile on the face of the man
or woman next in line. It scares me.
But then again, they were thinking of Heaven
and all it had to offer. They were leaving behind
the rotting bodies of the living
the way the man in the mural
on the opposite wall is not descending
but ascending into the warmth of the sky,
surrounded by his true friends
who are not afraid in the circle of light
to gaze up at him with love,
the only ones capable of seeing past
what little we've been offered—maybe
because there was only so much room:
two feet with sandals
two shins cut off at the ceiling.

Your Ad Says You Need a Well-Rounded Person

I can assure you that I've definitely
gotten around, and I love to work with language.
I know how to hit the head on the nail,
pull the hat out of a rabbit, and find
a rainbow at the end of a pot of gold.
Once, I even led water to a horse.
But I'm also a people person. The other day,
when I heard the toll-booth lady
say to the toll-booth man, *my arm hurts*,
I got out of my car, and among the protestations
of horns and curses in that lane,
gave her a full-body massage, working especially
on her tight, enormous calves.
I didn't laugh off her absurd tokens of pain,
like this guy named Teddy riding in the backseat.
I'd let him hitch with me and was talking
about a night hiking in the Alps.
I'd just gotten to the part of the story
where I had a few lines of Roethke,
when he grabbed all my maps and bailed out.
Lately, I've gotten better at digressing.
You might say I'm sort of a jack-in-the-box,
but if you did I wouldn't know what you mean.
I might as well tell you, I have limitations:
I never could get that water to drink the horse.
But I am perfect for the job. In the morning
I'm qualified to close my eyes and wrap
a maroon-striped pillow around my head,
to feel the light slowly brighten
in whichever room I happen to wake,
to wait for something metaphorical.

Victoria Raschke

The Seventh Day

Small. The stars are small, hard
cold like knowing mirrors sewn
into the pleated fabric of a woman's skirt.
They are alone here under them
his breath warm and moist against the curve of her.
How difficult is it to conceive below these wide-eyed suns?
There is something inside her empty with wanting,
crying out every time she starts to bleed.
It isn't that he knows this
or even wants it. It's her.
This need to create a new being whole, warm.
It's that she's only loved near him.
It's being afraid to die, without
screaming that creation,
feeling blood hot on her legs.
Now with him inside her
she feels real with the possibility that between
some spark is forming,
growing into her mother's laugh,
her father's dark eyes.

Breaking Bread

I.
I shred the dark leaves of spinach
with the honed edge of my favorite knife,
rocking it on the cutting board
in smooth, pulling strokes,
slide the thin ribbons off the wood
into the soup faintly glowing with saffron.

It is quiet in the kitchen, the house.
Outside the leaves churn ahead of the wind
in quick eddies on the lawn.
Later, the friends will come, bringing the wine,
and we will eat, laughing.

But now, it is the yearly ritual,
finding the perfect sweet potatoes
and acorn squash in the market,
soaking the dry chick peas the day before,
washing and washing and washing
the sand from the greens,
chopping the last of summer's tomatoes,
enjoying the liminal time between seasons
when the perishable summer fruits
and the autumn yield for keeping overlap,
scanning the stained recipe card
while my kitchen fills
with the scent of the fall soup,
a meditation just for me.

II.
Sitting alone
eating a bagel on the steps
outside my office,
I thought of M.F.K. Fisher
living alone in Last House,

the cottage her friend built for her,
and eating breakfast alone
after a life of fine food and conversation,
frying an egg in a little sweet butter
to eat with a piece of toasted peasant bread
from the market up the road and
maybe a spoonful of blackberry jam from summer.
Her own ritual uninterrupted by chatter
or a finicky child's request for something different.
If I were a condemned woman,
despite my love of ripe mangoes
sectioned in the skin, messily eaten,
and the perfectly bubbled autumn soup,
each ingredient added
at precisely the right time,
for my last meal,
I would request company.

Terry Olsen

The Language of Hua

Loving a flower and liking the flower
more than the feeling of being lost
in its language is the best I can hope
for when I hear you talk of your love

for me. Why one flower gives you my heart,
why three flowers define "I love you," why
nine hundred and ninety-nine flowers draw us
husband and wife, why eleven flowers shape

perfect this language between us I must
know. Why I drink your uncle's rose tea with-
out you, and you drink without me and your
flowers for my 30th birthday talked me silent.

Evening

My walk dangles.
I am king.

I am nothing,
but beginning

of where teeth stain,
and chip at holes.

I must bend.
You see yet

don't leave.
Love is too

much weight is
my thought of how

this does not
hurt but guess

it must.

Bradley Paul

Wide Is the Gate, Narrow the Way

Tour bus on a high narrow road.
Amalfi.
Driver got too casual,
too Italian.
Cell phone, cigarette.
Rolls the bus.
Now everyone will die
earlier than they thought.
Upside down, too.
Except as they fall
one man is already dead.
Died just after boarding.
Looked asleep.
A corpse on tour
over the lemon terraces
now tumbling
in a busful of corpses-soon-to-be.
He feels a bit of seniority and smiles
in that immobile corpse way.
My eternity, he thinks,
will forever be a half hour
longer than theirs.

Anybody Can Write a Poem

I am arguing with an idiot online.
He says anybody can write a poem.
I say some people are afraid to speak.
I say some people are *ashamed* to speak.
If they said the pronoun "I"
they would find themselves floating
in the black Atlantic
and a woman would swim by, completely
dry, in a rose chiffon shirt,
until the ashamed person says her name
and the woman becomes wet and drowns
and her face turns to flayed ragged pulp,
white in the black water.
He says that he'd still write
even if someone cut off both his hands.
As if it were the hands that make a poem,
I say. I say what if someone cut out
whatever brain or gut or loin or heart
that lets you say hey, over here, listen,
I have something to tell you all,
I'm *different*.
As an example I mention my mother
who loved that I write poems
and am such a wonderful genius.
And then I delete the comment
because my mother wanted no part of this or any
argument, because "Who am I
to say whatever?"
Once on a grade school form
I entered her job as *hairwasher*.
She saw the form and was embarrassed and mad.
"You should have put *receptionist*."
But she didn't change it.
The last word she ever said was No.

And now here she is in my poem,
so proud of her idiot son,
who presumes to speak for a woman
who wants to tell him to shut up, but can't.

Sarah Wagner

The Best Lesson Chemo Taught Me

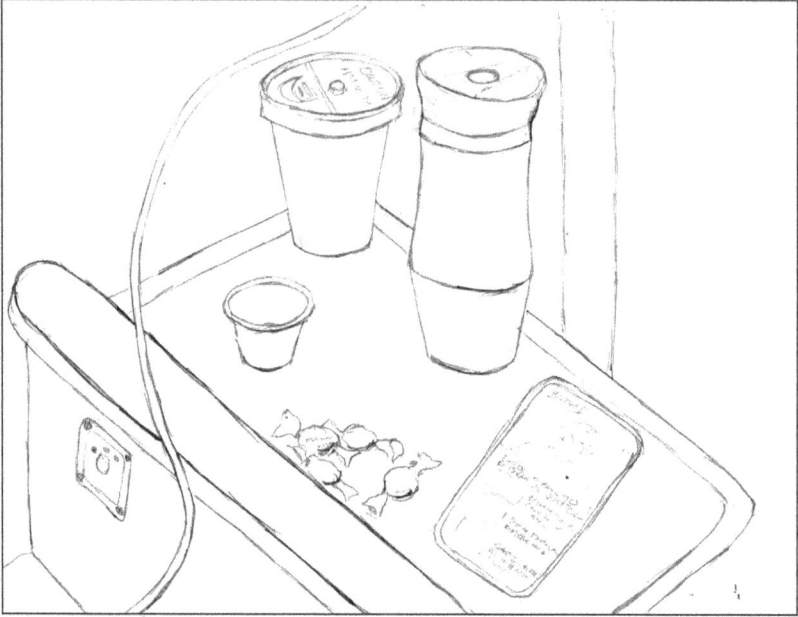

From a macro perspective, I was experiencing a great, albeit painful, lived metaphor: I knew that I was putting a toxin into my body and then I got to feel it leave.

I   got   to   feel   it   leave!

It was so beautiful!

There

was

a

beginning

and an

end

to

the pain.

With chemo, you know that you are putting toxic stuff in your body and that it will make you feel bad. On the other hand, the toxic chemicals I worked with*, and toxic relationships I sometimes got into, came into me with little pain and sometimes without my knowledge.

Toxins can be invisible and build up without you even knowing they are there.

It's that old saying about when you put a frog into a boiling pot of water it will jump out but put the same frog into room temperature water and bring it to a boil the frog will cook.

I had felt so exhausted for around three years, my breathing was weird and I knew something was wrong, I went to my doctor and he tried to help, and we did find a minor hole in my heart, but nothing to explain my symptoms other than menopause. My doctor put me on antidepressants

But the problem had been c a n c e r.

Then, when the tumor was cut out,

*Construction and art are two industries with a lot of exposure to toxins

                                              I
                                           felt
                                        really,
                                        really,
                                        really,
                                         good.

Underneath the pain of the wounds and the chemo,

                                 I felt normal,

                                 I felt healthy,

                                 I felt strong.

It was a great physical, experiential, metaphor for how I
                      don't want toxicity in my life.

                            I don't want to hurt.

                           I want to feel good.

              The best lesson chemo taught me is:

How good it

feels for

poison

to leave

my body.

Julia Beach

Danzig 1661

One was in love and carried a bird's nest
in the cavity where his heart should've been found.
All have eggs growing in their lungs.
Some will hatch into birds that sing
from broken ribs. Some will hatch
into locusts that eat the body into remains.

In the square a thousand others remained
hypnotized by the sky where seven sundogs nested.
Three in white, three washed in the stain of hatched
eggs, and one real with tapering tails found
rushing toward collision like a song
swelling up from Tuburculose lungs.

One was in love and fell mid-lunge
into repose, forever toward, to remain
unrealized. One became a song.
Three built a well-pitched nest
out of One's ribs. One would find
it romantic. Three sang to the hatchling

halos circling the sun. Hatch,
my sweet, said Another. My lungs
are tired of holding down. If I am found
at the end, let my hands remain
empty, One begged. Atop tower nest
the Faithful strike bells into song

hoping hope will blur the sky, singing
blues into indigo, indigo into violets that hatch
rainbows—both prism and prison—nestled
in the sky. Crack, crack, crack goes the red-eyed lung.
The eggs take a last remaining
breath as the body begins to founder.

One could not say he found
any of this romantic, apart from the singing.
Crack. Crack. Crack. Razor mouthed remainders,
faithful Plague Locusts, perihelion hatchlings
keen from an almighty lung
hallowed and hollowed like a nest.

The faithful find comfort in the nest
that sings, in lungs
that hatch and crack, crack, crack the remains.

In the Garden of Dread Reply

She wanders into the wild
carrying scissors

in her mouth, shrugs
the narrow shoulder

of stillness for the pleasure
of watching willow warblers

startle from cup-shaped nests
while searching

for telltale signs
of postcards on hedgerow bottoms.

A stamp that planted roots.
A salutation that slipped

its boots in the rain
and arrived with one wet sock.

Of all seasons, spring is most
cupboard mimic

where days arrange like shelves
broad with purpose

at the end of winter's purge.
Freshly the wind

carries the Penny Blacks
to the orchard canopy

to find perch
between God and the ground

to deliver from the void
something more than

lost something, some wild thing
astray with need.

Paul Guest

All I Know

The Statue of Liberty was crated in lentils
when shipped from France
and there is a species of catfish with scales
so tough piranhas can't get through
to soft meat. I'm thinking of what is vital,
today. The willow tree in my dreams that sways.
A little girl singing quiet approximations of hymns.
To the night. To the flames which are
tragic and kinetic and aren't ever receding.
The other day I was looking out over
what I believe was a river—forgive me
for not knowing the taxonomies of water—
and it was all noise, which is good
for some who struggle to sleep
or forget or change or learn or have any time
that isn't quilted with pain.
I was attempting to memorize the wet folds flowing by,
imagining the smoothness of rock
that was hidden beneath it all,
and composing another version of this poem.
One which has no complaint
inside its heart. No unanswered questions.
No bitterness for how it's turned out,
this life. My own. In the news this morning:
the death of a very great baseball player
and I shouldn't be so sad, I know.
Not when I'm agreeing with the girl in the elevator
that we have decades left, maybe,
before the world becomes even more of an irredeemable hellscape.
Before we're nostalgic for the Kardashians.
Because it wasn't so bad, then,
when nobody was heaving up
the bloody rags of their lungs
and nobody had figured out how to clone Henry Kissinger.

I have never figured out
what happiness is
or how to be in it. Never learned what is behind
door number three. If I want
a better life. If at this point one is even possible.
If this desperation is viral. If my name is good at any door.
I don't think so, not tonight, when
I'm trying to pretend that winter isn't real
and there are trees which glow
in the night and insects that sing beneath the light
of the moon. O alternate heart:
who could I be in another life,
and upon whom could I visit harm
like a storm? To dream of potency
is to write this poem and feel no pain whatsoever.
Remember me, I'm always saying
to the air as if it were listening,
sympathetic, capable of the idea of mercy.
One summer I taught myself
how to announce in Latin
to the world that I wanted nothing at all.
When, in truth, I was desperate
to be heard, understood, loved, my name a warm memory.
There was the wind and the ocean
and in it there were whales
that lowed in the darkness like the onset of collapse.
There was this dark will
and what could I say but my name and what hurt?

Karri Paul

Index
(utensils)

Identify the boring artifacts:
dirty bones and enemy souls
wooden among a tree's leaves

expect the scandal:
different tobacco different
trapdoor alone horny adequately

greet the "big-man"
by the handful
by the beautiful diameter

he decorates it hanging
documentation to prove it:
white pearl patterns

attract fertilize extract
do not fade or deteriorate
plant another tree

its worn clay shell
like the most basic wooden spoon
discarding every fruit

Photographic Sources

That red animal currency
grew out widely hung necklaces
purple pearl strings

what iridescence
what fierce body paint
the simplest crescents

a final beginning
both freshwater and sea
totally reddish exactly the

black-lettered manuscript stripped
of all poetry all parchment
seemed to have another

story in mind
that I should be telling
and it wouldn't hurt

Teresa Rogerson

Three haiku

anticipation
takes up all the space inside
desire fills the room

~~

the color of fire
marks the memory like flame
burnishes the tree

~~

we're able to smile
our hearts beat throughout our lives
how is this not great?

Magdelyn Hammond Helwig

Artemesia Gentileschi Painting Judith

When my father let him take me away,
not as prisoner, but as wife, it was the first time
I thought of you easing your fingers in Holofernes'

black hair, pulling the head back so his knotty white
neck jutted up like an unmarred landscape, so his face
was facing yours and the cool pressure of the sword.

You came for me like this at night, took my hand
and traced the path of blade across skin. When I
could not last, and left, I still could not escape you.

Each night, the sword, the bulging vein, the arc
of blood smudged across my canvas. I made your body
as round and strong as my own. Seducer and killer,

in my dark room, you never let me work alone,
your hand easing into mine, these slashes,
my brush, tender and tangled.

Laurel Snyder

The Mouse

Once there was a mouse. She lived and ate seeds. When the wind would and the rain, the mouse would and the rain. A mouse does, you know.

Once there was a mouse. A field of a mouse. Brown as quiet. Fall and the mouse was thin, too thin. The mouse went a scamper. The mouse met.

The mouse chattered and the magpies, from their posts. The farmer opened a door. The mouse had never heard of a door, heard a door. The mouse crept.

The farmer and the magpies were too much with the mouse. The farmer was warm. He steamed in the morning. The door was a hole in the picture.

Not *his* picture. The mouse knew holes, knew steam, but. The mouse was tired, crawled into a puddle behind a shed. Waited for something. The mouse.

Not *the* shed. Not *the* puddle. The mouse, crying, small, wanted a seed. The shed weathered storms. Whiskers said the seeds were elsewhere.

The bones were too small to be noticed. The farmer's feet were large. It had been two seasons. Picked clean and quiet. *So* the mouse was planted.

Dear Nostalgia,

Where to begin? Mildew on a pillow. The grit of the gray Atlantic four days in my hair. Scratchy radio. Happiness.

Long-gone skin, smooth and dirty. The stink of fireflies dead on my hands. Stolen wine. French fries with boredom. Ketchup. And the music of—

Rooftops and whiskey, the cat box in the corner. Jasmine through the window. Voices like rust and fiddles.

My own my own my own. Plaintive soundtrack to the movie of my *then*. How I've needed you. How I've carried you. How I've cultivated your tendrils.

My kudzu my love. At the end of it all, there you are. Decorating the worst, choking my dull world into your lovely green distraction.

I cannot tell anymore what you are strangling, and what you are holding together.

Laura E Howard

My Own Slovenia

There are weddings on Saturdays in Bled, Slovenia.
Cars with cans and streamers come flying
off the back road from the Alps.
I'm not sure which church they use for the ceremonies.
I imagine them getting married in the church
with the wooden head of St. John the Baptist from 1380.

Two artists, father and son, have a studio next door to the Pletna.
Boris tells me how his father rides into town at nighttime
on a motorcycle with a broken headlight.
One night in May, the son invites me over to see his paintings.
He motions towards the walls with dirty hands.
I am careful to step around his father's sculptures made
        from shrapnel.

I think of my brother telling about the day and night
he spent in a bar near the Croatian border.
How he heard the sounds of shelling while he drank his pivo,
Now, years later, I stand here and try to picture him in this bar,
his right front tooth missing, how he tried to write his
        own Slovenia,
starting with the *Dance of Death* fresco in the church in Hrastovlje.
The last skeleton in the fresco holds a list of those coming along—
a nun, a queen, a child, it didn't matter who you were.

Standing in the store beside the house in Bled,
I only know the Slovenian words for tomatoes,
for bread, for cheese. I point to a round loaf
and think of the candle shaped like an angel
that I got my mother from the bee-keeping museum in Radovljica.
I chipped one of the angel's wings right after I bought it—
fragile corners of beeswax jutting from an otherwise stable body.

Tiny Glasses Full of Gin

Because you told me I could never be faithful,
I tried to sit in one spot on one bench in the Luxembourg Gardens,
while reading one single page of Colette's *The Last of Chéri*.
The water in the Fontaine Médicis was silent and still,
but the gods were still there, hovering, sculpted from stone.
Soon, my mind began to wander.
I wrote a story about a character who is obsessed with arms.
In the garden, I saw all sorts of arms—
short arms, hairy arms, arms with bracelets, arms without passion.
One night, you stole for me—
a wheelbarrow from a construction site on a back street.
We were all dressed up from a cheap Chinese dinner
and fortunately, you found an old couch cushion thrown out
        in an alley
and it padded the chunks of plaster still in the bottom.
I had saved my free fold-out fan from dinner.
So, riding in my air-conditioned wheelbarrow,
with you holding all the weight, I lost my voice in between
        my laughter,
like a short period of silence followed by something that is not
silent. My lack of words became an established room,
a bar just for men and their cigars,
their tiny glasses full of gin and fancy. And sometimes,
sometimes, I think of that creaking door of the car you used to
        pick me up in.
Somehow, you always lead me back here, stuck
        between narratives.

Melanie Jordan

Charlie Brown in the Dead of Night

This howling makes me shiver, but it ought to be beautiful.
I wish he would stop. And you're out there, too,
little girl, smiling over sticker albums and apple slices.
Who takes care of us? Who mends trees
when their limbs crack, who thinks of a question like that?
I know worry is a way of filing, but the folders are too long
or too narrow and none of my frets ever fit. The space
around my head at night is easier to work with,
blankets piled on top of me so I can barely see the rise
of my chest. They don't mend them, that's who.
I don't know which is worse, the barking or the silence.
Tomorrow, maybe, I can win your eye
with animal crackers or a pencil with sparkling foil clefs.
And what good is that, the blessing eye that might not see
me surrounded by autumn's energy and nearly bursting
with rhapsodic blood? It's a lot to look for.
There's a lot to see in people, the way they hover
at the edge of knowing and oblivion, the way they keep on
clipping hair and making appointments, clocks with hearts.
It's definitely a tick when I see you, your dress smoothed
over invisible knees, tick the way I feel you know me.
I've danced with girls before, swaying lightly back
and forth, just on the edge of what it means
to fill my body, of being poured in like wet cement.
Then worry fills my shoes, but it's almost pretty,
a haze like sundown or chiffon before I have to sit down.
If life is a series of escapes to the punchbowl, I want to ask
out loud, is this it? But what kind of question is *that?*
I'll be fixed tomorrow when the day is mine, opened up
like the white cream of a cookie. Keep trading
lunches and mittens with me—what is love but one
big cloakroom—because mine is the longing
of a Hercules let loose, mine is the fear of a burst

oil candle, bright with flame and dim with the rupture.
He'll keep it up. Until I'm out there barefoot
with flashlight and dogdish, or until sunlight sticks up
unruly, ready as a willing head waiting to be combed.

The Kiss of the Cage

Only a block or so to visit him, the sculpture
seated like a man: birdcage for a torso,
gangling legs in littletramp shoes. Funny

how the docents watch me, carefully unobservant,
make sure I'm no defiler, no bomb.
They watch me so long, drift away.

Magritte's *Healer* can't leave me, not even
with his cane. I start with it, my pen
sketching, parceling him new proportion,

scratching the ink of my poor art onto the page
as late fuchsia petals stitch the sidewalk outside
my museum. They will come back

like black branches crowding a house. This summer,
my father stood watch while I slept, to make sure
I was breathing, maybe, to make sure I wouldn't

take pills, die in the night with the bottle
or some new defeat. Really, though, the worst
had passed; I'd only been sapping the gallery,

regular as a junkie, not sure at first
what pulled me to the bronze and satchel
of a hollow man, to the cloaked cage

we're all made of, but his body gapes;
air passes clean through. With no head,
he opens like a temple bell.

So here I stand, ask, dare; I smile
sometimes from the pressure, amused at the two
silhouettes on the blank gallery wall,

happy raconteurs. Whatever poison is urned
in me burns like a floe. It looks for exit
from my catacombed head. I'm a room

with eight walls. I'm an ancestor asking
him to trepan. The ember moves up my spine;
I can feel him at the core, feel the thumping

call from my own chest, regular, meaning
I'm still here I'm still here

like a droplet of glass next to its lover,
a cracked window glittering the earth. The bird

could be hobbled, the way it hovers there on edge.
But it isn't. She meets her double

there, and the kiss of the cage which is always open.

Ever Saskya

The Horrible Life I Could Have Had

For Richard Jackson

My father tried to kill us.

We survived him   where dandelions and marigolds feed   the newer flowers
      form our skin   and bones.
          Where the earth is
          moist and tempted,
     and we   bury people.

My father tried to kill me,   and no one believed me.

What does it mean to be believed?
With your skin straight up against the sky,
The earth moves again—I'm sure of it—
With our bones landing
Before we are blown down.

To Him: "I don't   remember you   lovingly."

We had so much to do in life   more than running   and running the sadness.

He is dead.   We are free

Does the earth hurt   when we bury people in it?
                    Does it ask:
                    "Is the body taken?"
                    Should I vomit on his bones?
                    Should I pull the roots to check for sure?

We only borrow these bodies for so long,
the known   and the unknown
visit us   in all the lights
            that matter.

I tried
to erase   all the lightning,
                        but I could not
                        discard it from myself.

Then, Rick said,
            you are all the lights that matter;   you are you and,
            "You need to get out of this town,"   move the sky,
            tell the storms that wake us,   "I will help you."

That is   what it means   to be believed:
                                        Yellow   breaches the trees,
                                running and running and running.

Opening the Mouths of Trees

My brother would take me to the river.
We would watch the water around rocks move
hard over stone, push dirt into banks—

on the ground the river walks;
steps across the land in inches, ankles
pulling against earth's urge for retention.

But the world changes in dimension, shadow,
clouds fold over us like the roof
of our parents' house.

(Green walls gathered curtains by the windows. I waited,

the woods outside, the river
like a bending elbow around the land.) Brother's voice
calls water into the ground,
opening the mouths of trees.

It's a good day for rain.
It's a good day—let the world fall down.

TC Tolbert

Imago Dei

This is where the shout of someone else's hands is planted. Inside
stillness. Inside a small light near what is hidden.
Thinking, always, implies the body can be outgrown. Or at least
become a light in which to hide.

To remove you from view was initially a relief, Melissa. I wonder
if every word is a lie by omission. Furniture, I believe,
is still in conversation with the forest. Paper too. I am listening for
what each word, even whispered, wants to hide.

Trans. Queer. White. Passing. Who you have become outside of
your old names, Melissa. Missy. Moe. So many shears still inside.
Verbally, physically, sexually abused. As a child. As an I. Here is a
self-portrait as a hiding, ongoing, underneath the hide.

Now I sleep with a pillow on my chest. Before God, I wear wool,
linen, nylon, and polyester blends. Also MagiCotton™.
And CyberSkin™. Every body I dream in needs pressure of some
kind to create breath from outside. May we all hide

a little more air in our lungs. The kind that gives flight to flame.
The kind that buries fire in the tongue. I love you who cannot be
touched. May the small work of speaking be enough to shake God
from her cage. To protect us. In plain sight we are. She is hiding.

In the outsized chest. In the chest etched with T. In the chest so flat
one cannot grasp the light stunning what's inside. I praise
every chest and what a chest could be made of. The makers of
chests. And those who make this more lovely. Living inside a hide.

[untitled]

A man's arms may trick his shadow—Melissa—may become the open

chamber he longs to live inside—held in the lungs of another—

what unforetold music may emerge even from the hair of a horse

stretched between two bent ends of a Pernambuco stick and then rubbed

against a dried and twisted selection of a young sheep's gut—it is 2020

and every day now the world's windows rattle—sunrise, that relentless bastard, still

searches the dirt for what has the potential to explode—what cannot become louder larger

if only by eventually allowing itself to be slammed shut—perhaps this is another way of singing into

every day's disappearance—enlarging what survives—without justification—here I am having

never learned how to keep (this too the work of every beating body) time—what if we did not

suspect the dead of going on somewhere without us—would we call our own names—if we knew

the very wind pushing through each fence, each room was to be remembered

as another's expelled breath—silent—looking at you now, shaping
sound strikes me as

departure practice—lifting up from the shoulders a little—listening
for the measure marked

tacet—wave after wave expanding against one another—
underneath loss lives touch—

A straw-haired
broom
holds the hollow
door open—every
bird I see I say please
do not hear me—
I never felt
what I feel
a line could be—
my fear has made me
small—rain
on an ox
eye—a pigeon wet
with its own
name—the bell inside
a metal bowl struck
and then set loose
by a rock

Poem in search of comfort—

Keith Driver

In the City Where Everyone Is Crying

In the city where everyone is crying there is a chalky tower. There is a portly chapel with a red tile roof. There is a computer store open two days a week. The names of the city council members sound like seawind through the seagrass. In the city where everyone is crying the pedestrian zone permits small truck traffic. There is an old city wall and beyond the old city wall is the new City Where Everyone Is Crying in a Shopping Mall or Gastropub. The official tree is the Linden tree in the City Where Everyone is Crying.

I found no linden trees in the City Where Everyone Is Crying. When I was there I saw a doctor whose name was the word for lumber. My torso was diagnostically irradiated. In the City Where Everyone Is Crying, I took a walk by the historically significant river. I drank a mélange in a cafe with mirrored walls. I may have been the only person there.

In the City of Uniformed Children

In the City of Uniformed Children everyone is pledging allegiance to something. Everything has a flag and a slogan. The high school is a granite coliseum. The sky is hot and low and the tops of the taller buildings are dusted with its chappy skin. The center of the City of Uniformed Children is braceleted with elevated highways under which live some of the citizens of the City of Uniformed Children. In tents. Or wrapped in mildewed tarps, where, just like everywhere else, they receive their being from locations and not from space.

When I went to the City of Uniformed Children, I made a clearing in the plains and called it a space. A space is something that has been made room for within a boundary. The space joined with its boundary. I built a small bridge there out of wax and mud and the tall sand-colored grass of the plains. The bridge crossed the boundary. In the City of Uniformed Children, there is a precinct for institutions where the uniformed children live, a precinct for industry where they bake bricks and melt iron, and a train yard, which is an open wound in the middle of staying.

[untitled]

A statue, an inescapable she. The myth of birth, and love, and war, and wisdom. Statue of Eve minus Adam, the flesh of a red velvet chaise, flesh of a death wrap, flesh of a wound before the blood fills. With a mammal's vertical spine, a statue plus her mirrored image board an ark. A Latin genus, a Greek goddess, a to-be-named hurricane. A city-state statue, fires burning plot-by-plot, an amphitheater to carry the sounds of angry crowds. Statue of cherub, of cupid, of creepy flying creatures. After having witnessed the crusades she sleeps through the century of revolutions. A throne-seated princess hears wishes close-up. Lady-in-waiting fluffing pillows in malaise. A Darwinian statue choosing which child to keep. Her skin a baker's fondit rolled out to glaze a wedding cake, a butterfly's wing held by forceps. Daughter of memory, the statue forgets to walk her dog. A birdbath, a looted urn from an Iraqi palace, a half-horse hood ornament. A statue inside an egg inside a basket, inside the black box of a plane. Statue of a country western song, the white mouth of a ceiling, statue of snowflakes that do not melt on the tongue. She has a front and back, a beginning, but no end. Her feet rest in a file of "Missing Objects." She needs no help undressing. A statue lives in a garden, but basks *dans le jardin*. She, calcified from the breast of a breast. What is the opposite of apocalypse? She is a statue of that.

[untitled]

It is summer and we are on the illusion of vacation. A brief evening breeze breaks up the mosquitoes. You've been there. And by summer, I mean an awareness of what will not keep. Because it is the season to bleed, I write everything out in pencil. My confessions of guilt, my experiments on behavior: we base the physics of our travel on a desire to leave, which is negated by the desire to stay. Eventually they cancel each other out and we are sweating on a bench.

I learned from a good thief that the trick to stealing is to believe the object already belongs to you. How could I lift the muse from her pedestal? Could I carry her through the swivel door without knocking off her shoulder or triggering an alarm?

Once I stole sunflowers from summer. I whacked a Weed Eater along a fence line cutting the flowers at their shins. I arranged the corpulent stalks in an umbrella stand. I sat the stand in front of a fireplace swept clean of ash. When a visitor complimented the freshness of the flowers, I told her I bought them from a florist. When she asked which florist, I said the criminal one. By criminal, I mean an unauthorized transaction between two souls.

Rachel Morgan

Child-Sized Pastoral

The cornfields rise
like a sloping sea floor.

There's enough sky
to exceed the late morning.

There's farms,
but no farmers.

It's seven turns
over two hours

until the children's
hospital, where you

announce our arrival
in the city of towers!

full of potions, and
needles we pretend swords.

After each visit, we exit
the parking garage

into a kingdom
of endangered prairie

whose only protector
is its destroyer. In the dark,

there's nothing to see,
but you look out the window

and tell me you see birds,
hear a song that goes like

These Mountains

You might tell yourself you want to leave, and you do—
you leave, in your twenties for a coast, for a man,

the next decades you visit the sagging porch, dad's cough,
red-spotted salamanders, muddy oracles of the mountain.

Your grandfather taught you which grapevines to swing,
how to brew mountain tea, tie string to a June bug's leg.

He's memory now, visits as dappled sun through trees,
porch swings, a laugh that rumbles and cracks.

In the kitchen, Dolly's song *My Tennessee Mountain Home*
blisses from the speakers. Its earnestness catches

you off guard. Your therapist says we remember more
bad things than good, to protect our future selves.

Your lyric-filled heart, heavy on the vine, sodden with
experience is suddenly blithe. The July ditches wave

with orange lilies, each their own little sun orbiting
eloquent stems as cars eclipse. It happens now, a moment

poofs to memory—to dwell on something becomes a dwelling,
constantly constructing the cabin where you lived and live.

Caroline Klocksiem

Reading *The Declarative Language Handbook: Using a Thoughtful Language Style to Help Kids with Social Learning Challenges Feel Competent, Connected, and Understood* at the CSL Plasma Donation Center

Did you see the blood
moon last night I ask the phlebotomist. I'm allowed

to get stuck after passing
the usual intake questions

(Am I feeling healthy today
In eight weeks will I live
where I do now

Do I understand
        risks
        medications
        consent
        effects?)

                (Agree I guess?)

No
but I know
it was hot in the parking lot
at ten

like hot-hot
like BLAH hot.

Yeah.
My mindfulness

app asks one thing
I learned

this year. I input that Questions
might be a sort
of violence
to some of us. I learned
that Questions enrage

my son—they just extract
way way too much

        energy
simply by existing
a spiked alert that splatters
the clear
space of what had been
a softly quiet room, intrusive

claw of the Question mark
ripping through to spill
a choice, tangle air

into a flow chart

        to not respond ➡ or ➡ to respond

        ⬇   ⬇

      (?)   and   how / when / in what
way / with what

      language ➡

              spoken   { hollered
                                murmured
                                garbled

.

```
                              ┌ paper
             written       ─┤   freeform
                              └ type-to-text

                              ┌ glare
                              │ slumped
             body          ─┤   slow
                              │ hurled
                              └ stone
```

...I keep working
on processing

into declaration. Declaration ➝ *no action is required at this time*

        Like maybe
                I hope
                I wish
                I wonder

                                Little offerings draped across
                                a chair to be picked up or not

OK

        but

when I caught the blood moon
by instinct last night I admit
I yanked with glee unthinking
my family
out their screens, asking,
needing
them
to experience

that cursive light red light with me
those last few streaks of day settling to sleep
the way my delta waves playlist
never really stops but fades rather velvetly out

while the moon—that overflowing copper drum—
beats itself up
in a graying old light

a heart pulsing higher in the dark
of a throat
with each breath.

                Holding there, showing us

light.

Both my kids
have started saving

for a VR headset
                to share
                some liminal space together   to escape this one

reality we can barely afford
for one
for many
in which
they get

to craft for themselves
endless
vibrant
vital systems   ➡   whole parts

                              with
                              no Questions

Liz Marlow

Sara's Uniform

Majdanek, 1942

I wear these stripes—
streaks of tears through dirt,

a river's channels dry
where water once pushed

aside what stood in its way.
I wear shoes of bricks

pulled from a mausoleum.
As I lift a foot, which

descendant reveals their face—
imprint in gravel—what

could have been? I wear a halo
of smoke—sack

floating, hot air
balloon—on the platform,

hoping to land somewhere
I will see familiar faces.

Avraham on Freedom

Treblinka, August 2, 1943

Icarus's father, Daedalus, constructed wings out of peacock feathers
and melted yahrzeit candles from all their ancestors. He was tired of
the dead weighing him down—their memory in his name. He said
to Icarus, *With these wings, we can fly over the labyrinth that traps
us.* But when Icarus first tried on the wings, adjusting them on his
shoulders, their weight left an impression in his skin like a string tied
tight around a turtle's shell. He stood still for quite some time, staring
over the edge of the cliff at the labyrinth's perimeter, waiting on wind
to lift him. And then it happened—his father's push or a gust took
him (he didn't care which). For once, nothing was in his way, nothing
seemed like it could drag him down. The sun's warmth calmed him
like his mother's breath, but too much of anything can be a bad
thing. And just like that, as all his ancestors called his name through
the heat, he knew he would never really leave the labyrinth. Wings a
myth, but those yahrzeit candles real, and he realized in that moment,
the only possibility of freedom was jumping off the cliff.

Joshua Mensch

Prince Edward Island

I lost whatever I buried in the sand.
Summer after summer we'd return
to find it altered. Only the signs
remained where they'd been planted.
The ridges of grass rose or sank
by the storms that pushed the bank,
the ice floes punished and scraped.
In town, the ice cream parlour remained
my favourite event. I still don't know
how they made it, but if I tasted it again?
I have a way of ruining things.
Once, on the ferry over,
before they built the bridge,
my father poured soup from a thermos
and smiled as the other passengers looked on.
How cleverly he'd managed things.
The food on the ferry was bland.
The view was always the same.
I stood at the railing and watched
Prince Edward Island resolve
into a thick strip, with buildings and cars,
while behind us, Nova Scotia dissolved.
Being an unsteady child,
I often dropped things.
One time it was a camera.
No doubt the pictures it contained
were banal and largely out of focus,
the sea slanted at various angles,
glittering and pale. The antics
of my sister, my father grinning
with his wide moustache, a boy
with his eyes half closed.
Photos we'd look at once, while still
in the envelope, and then never again,

until many years later, perhaps
after our parents' deaths, sifting
through their lives and stopping
now and again to look and remark
the passage of time with regret.
Were those photos not lost
I would not remember them.
Had I seen them, I would not
regret their loss. This is the way:
Whatever I buried, whatever I dropped,
I kept somewhere.

Nova Scotia

In my dreams I am always falling,
and always from a great height.
Because it is a dream, I don't die,
but neither do I survive.
The dream wants me to fall
and then fall again.
It's interested in the moment I slip,
the moment I am pushed
from behind. There is acceptance,
I imagine, in falling, but my dream
doesn't want me to know about that.
My dream is interested
only in terror, the reaction of the heart.
Sometimes, though,
it's other people falling
and I'm the one trying to catch them.
Sometimes they're strangers,
sometimes they're people I've loved
in other dreams. People whose deaths
I fear more than my own,
so I reach out to catch them
but the dream pushes me out.
I'm like a dog at my dream's door,
panting and wagging to be let in.
My body hates this notion.
It roots me to the bed
to remind me all is well
and no one is falling.
No one fell.
My younger sister
staring over the sea
from an unstable ledge
above a sharp abundance of rocks
didn't fall,

nor did my wobbling mother:
atop the stones of an old ruin
my hand steadied her,
just as it caught my father
when the shale crumbled
underneath him
on the cliffs at Arisaig.
We came for the view
and the view was extraordinary.
But if you look closely
at my dream
you can see a pair of legs
sticking out of the water
where a man has fallen
and the ship he was on
steaming away into a beatific horizon.

Mark Bilbrey

The Dog of Conversation

Let's talk then about the self

Woof

Look

      The dog is sleeping

Like a windmill

The Dog of the Throat

Dear throat:

Given every living thing,

given the farmer's
          and butcher's slaughter

—in you are the hog's hearts,
the stalks, and the milk,
and the grains of the wind,
the grain heard, the flock herded,

the swallow, the holler—

what, throat, at your age,
given every sing

—and you cough and collapse
and hack clear a way
back through for so little
a cry as the flies make—

whose moan's still born?

Kristi Maxwell

KOALA

an extinction

different fires require different fixes
wetness isn't it every time

did Muir grieve missing species' preceding densities—
see their missingness   the edges' misgivings

perceive the un-
quinces didn't preserve

residues extend remembering—the tide
venturing in, the drying spume
its spine   the spirit vein deveined   deemed excess

we experienced judgment when wind whipped us

meted mischief by describing—
fruit is a tree's sequins

ruined by the bite
who isn't though

(get even, Eve)

is this triggering
this being minted by suffering

the minute (but this isn't time—try twice) the minute
the determining mini

teensy thing   the *seeming*

Note on form: This piece is part of a series of lipograms, writing that
excludes one or more letters. The poems take as their starting place the

names of endangered species and emerged out of a desire to manage my own climate despair. Specifically, I'm working with modified beautiful outlaws, which I've named "extinctions" (lipograms that do not use the letters in the subject's name—in this case, the name of the endangered species), to explore what happens when what is endangered is instead absent—gone. The formal strategy of the lipogram nods to the global trends regarding climate change and strategies of elimination (eliminating carbon emissions, red meat consumption, plastic, etc.).

from SCROLL

To eat Elvis, draw Elvis
on a cookie, then bite

To eat eyeless
men? A cartoonish submarine into which

no one may fit?

The image is all
that needs

changing

Slathered in streetlight

your painted cheek is pretty as snow

The outline you give your eye, as if it were
to draft itself

An essay on seeing

The manmade lens

The whole human in fact "manmade"
inside the bright lab of another body

Unfollow the turtle onto whom has been soldered wheels

There is a carrot yet to be peeled
A carrot yet to rot

despite a name's smuggling

A speed bump inside oneself

Get over it

To specify "goldenrod" or "canary"
To un-narrate a story   turning "I" into a slit
other words will sew up

Healing was bound to come
its little possum nose sowing night into the field
the moon disrobed

just earlier

while I sat looking for the poem

L.S. McKee

Alva and the Magnetic Resonance

There is a cage over her head
in the space chute the nurse

hummed her into, the nurse's hand
on Alva's knee until the very last

second, a gesture of kindness,
which almost made Alva cry

because she knew the nurse
was a mother to someone—

she could feel it in the weight
of the nurse's hand, this mothering,

this tiny gesture of: "as I push you
inside the machine, I will hold you

in the smallest way possible."
Alva lies inside on the electric

gurney. The doctor told her:
"a little swelling where the brain

meets the eye," so they must
"take a look" inside her.

In the waiting room, she'd sat
surrounded by doors, knowing

at the very moment, behind one,
someone was being dissected by light,

someone was being read by light.
And behind another, radiological

fortune-tellers divined hidden messages
written in bones or in gray orbs the size,

maybe, of sparrows' eggs: the prophecies
of science. The fates they measure.

Inside the MRI, Alva closes her eyes
to remember the boundaries of her sight

are still intact. The room with the nurse
is haloed around her feet. The nurse's hand,

gone, turns the machine on.
Suddenly, everything is washed away

by sound. A woodpecker thumps, calls
across a forest of white trees, bleached

by the diagnostic sun. Alva floats in a lake
of echoes. Then a hammering. A pulse winds

faster. Inside the machine, she knows,
magnets spin in short, engineered orbits

to peel away layers, to see inside her.
It is a small consolation, to imagine

the technician, later, like a monk, will study
his illuminated manuscript, the parts

of her body no one else will see,
another way of being held.

Alva on Getting Dumped in the Desert

It was the last home she'd chosen
for herself, though the air gave her
nosebleeds: blood suddenly on the

sofa pillows—a few drops that would
never wind their way back to the heart.
But still. The air made her bleed.

The desert sky a low ceiling. The altitude
of the city higher than the mountains
of her hometown, where lush trees

clambered up the slopes. When he'd taken her
to the desert for the first time, she'd reached
to pet a prickly pear that grew from the sidewalk

like a balding animal. Dozens of hair-thin
needles impaled in her skin, too tiny to pull free.
Shaking his head at her idiocy: "Why in the world?"

And Alva replying: "they had looked soft."
You might think this is a metaphor for the worst
of love. For the wrong men that made

her right. But it's not. He knew the remedies
of the region, and in the bathroom of their rental,
he put down the lid of the toilet to be eye level

with her wounds: her hand cupped in his
as he unspooled the Scotch tape that would yank
the needles out, and she would know in that moment

there was no one else. For years it was truth
until it wasn't. Someone more beautiful,
though he didn't have to say it. She knew it

already, burning, as they stood on the balcony
of their condo whose walls were made of glass—
whole rooms in which they couldn't hide

from the desert, and so, stepped into it.

Jenny Sadre-Orafai

Testing a Pattern

I've watched someone who needed air
pitch a loose fist through her own window.
It was the second time I watched her die.

My mouth is a window open.

I hang heavy toile curtains—a scene
of a shepherd carrying an animal dead
upside down. Its lungs are closed.

You see it if you look for it.

I wake up every morning surprised
I'm alive. My breastbone pops, an instrument
warming up. If I said, there's more living

than dying. If I said, it's easier to surrender.

The way my mother's hand holds the back
of my father's seat in the car when
she pulls out of a parking space

and how he flinches like he can feel it.

Swim, Swam, Swum

They locked me in—a string of boys
lining four rows of corn and their smiles

pushing against the stalks, bright
and polished. The stars were on.

To feel the crop crash against a body
that belonged, that I didn't want—

their shoulders, white, shoving
their way through the air.

His cheeks, red or pink
from youth or embarrassment. Was he

embarrassed. Did he know what his hands
shouldn't do. Did one of them hesitate.

I learned how to close
off when I was six, how to swim out.

Taylor Loy

Work

All we do is dig,
keep our shovels moving.
Move earth, mound it up,
carve it with dull blades
of prayer. You don't need faith
to move a mountain;
You make it something else,
something less real.
Something you couldn't believe
unless you laid your hands on it.
This was what my father taught me
that God meant. That the real test
was the labor of Isaac,
how he must have known
that we build our deaths
on obedience—we work
though, as the ram works to free itself
from the thicket. In these ditches
we dig out foundations,
we dig paths for water, we dig
basements, places for underpinning,
we dig out trenches, we dig quiet
places of rest, all six feet of grandfather's grave,
we dig when our shovels hit clay,
we dig for fear of rain, we dig
to free ourselves. We dig
to point toward a hill and exclaim
   we worked there—
That God may have made this world,
but we work like hell to make it ours.

Construction Site, an approach to therapy

I'd rather be pouring concrete. If only
to wake up mornings with a simple answer
for every ache—to separate
this day's body from the last.
To dismiss the myth that we survive
our sleep.

The wooden form is reassuring.
Itself a stabilizing, a holding in of weight
only to be knocked away when it becomes
merely a holding on—when the wood's strength
becomes the weak home of termites
colonizing the crawlspace.

In Glasgow, Charles Rennie Mackintosh
built a school of art of concrete
polished so smooth that you'd swear
it was marble.
                        Inside, he built a library
from a forest—a garden enclosed
in concrete. A second Eden
where we, the damned, are free to eat.

Is it wrong to exalt this work, this toiling
under the sun? The building of towers,
the laying of foundations, the moving of stones
from one place to the other.

Kelly Moore

An Alternate Ending to My Affair with Mr. Blank (II)

He had the longest beak I'd ever seen on a man.

On a sunny afternoon, we drank our coffee
laughing at the mess we'd made of the sugar packets.

"Is nothing sacred?" I teased as he pecked a hole in my Splenda
and swung it around in the air.

Outside, the cars were dashing over a hill.

"Those are dolphins," he said,
"jumping over the brown, malodorous waves.
A sign of luck on the ugliest day in the world."

"Is this a poem," I asked, "or are you talking to me?"

"What kind of a world do we live in," he said,
"that we can't read anything for what it really is?"

I said, "You have the most symmetrical face
I've ever seen on a man. I could fit
my face inside it perfectly." (He darted his eyes,
hid his beak inside his cup of coffee.)
"I want all of you," I said.
"I want to smell the back of your tongue."

"You are strange," he said.

I said, "You're the one
with the beak," and the room went black.

He threw his head back. He swung open his beak.
I didn't know if it was an insult or an invitation.

He was an open trap door, a middle finger in the air, silent
for a good five minutes. I thought of the possibilities
of beak on breast, tail on ass, a blood-curdling caw,
a death, an image, a revelation.

One slat of light in the blinds sliced at my pupils,
and I grew tired of waiting for an ending. [12345678]

So I laughed, and I laughed so hard that my stomach
fell out of my mouth, and onto the table.

---

[1] "I can see your gizzard from here," I said. "What do you think I am? Your mother?"

[2] End on a disturbance, a diversion, an interruption.

[3] His poem about the dolphins should come true somehow.

[4] "And the front door must have opened because the air became heavy with the smell of the skin of the sea."

[5] "It was morning and the street was spilling in through the window. Carefully I pulled my foot out of his throat without waking him."

[6] The next morning doesn't matter.

[7] "So I stood up and bellowed into the bottom of his dark gullet, 'ORATORIO!'"

[8] "Outside, a bulldozer, cacophony of starlings, blind and swinging at any echo within reach."

The End of the Aquatic Apes

with lines from Zhuang-zi

1.

The bottom halves of people in the sea
                trail from them like squid ink.

I've seen how the water tricks
                the body out of itself.

Our legs wave about, thoughtless
                as we stare into the distance.

I hate the cold of entering the water, how
                the skin shrivels,
                                folds in all the chill.

2.

One day, we won't recognize our own limbs.

If tomorrow my left arm is transformed into a rooster,
                I'll go looking for night's end.

If my right arm turns into a crossbow,
                I'll hunt for owls to roast.

If my hips become a pair of wheels, if my shadow
                takes the form of a horse, I'll ride away—

3.

Who will carry us back to the water
                when the sun goes down?

Hay-on-Wye, the Trowley Farm

We grew accustomed to the constant
misting rain, the lonely shale abutments and green
sloping hills, the matted sheep, to falling
out of our wet clothes every night in the slatted farm
bed, while wind flung hard carols through the trees.
The one couple among fifteen other boarders,
my wife and I slept in what had once been the nursery,
the only room small enough for privacy,
and every night, when we set the lamps to burn
against the window's false mirrors and shut our crooked
oak door, we could pretend that our world
was here, in a rambling Welsh farmhouse,
two miles up from the Wye and its swans like strewn pearls.
We began neglecting the trips to town to stay
behind in the house alone. We watched the Welsh news,
warning of drought in a country that saw daily rain.
We watched a Queen concert and Beatles documentary
on VHS, left there by a previous tenant. Megan was cold
all the time, I drank too much, both of us sick
from poverty and cheap canned food.
We felt more at home than ever before.

There were two brown horses in a fenced pasture
beside the gravel lane that led to the farm.
During the day, they lingered near the farm, as if curious
about our domestic habits, what glimpses
they caught through the small, inset windows.
Maybe it is stupid to imagine, then or now as I
write this, that they had any interest in us, but we had never
lived near horses, and we were in love with them.
We stood in the rain for hours, rubbing their muddy flanks,
their warm black eyes washing over our faces,
bright from the cold wind. A flock of the ubiquitous
sheep shared their pasture, and one morning,

as my wife and I were walking past, the horses broke
into a sudden, jerking trot, straight through the placid
sheep, who as a body scattered, bleating frantically,
like robots in old science fiction films when their circuitry
overloads. And the horses turned to look at us,
whickering, stamping the dirt. Laughing, and inviting
us to join them. My wife and I young, longing
for something to cherish; it was good then to love
and be loved, good to be watched by those animals,
good to laugh at the sheep, while out on the moors
their wild horse ancestors kept their ways, flowing
like a river, neither evil nor kind in its motion, but good.

Aberystwyth

A loose line of gulls hovered over the shore,
dozens of them, battling the wind, then losing,
sweeping in narrow pale elliptics back toward
the green hills crowding the shore. I stood with my wife
and a few friends, picking smooth stones from the beach
for keepsakes when we got back home. The waves frothed
over like packs of mad dogs, whipped by the wind.
I wanted to stand and stare into its dark,
furious heart, steady as the gulls, who bore
their defeat tenaciously, always swimming
back through the wind to mark the tide's swirling line
with their bodies, to stare into the roiling,
tearing sea, but that cold everlasting gale
was too much. We slipped into the thin alleys
that curled back into the city. Hard faces
turned to us in the café but looked away,
uninterested—faces made for staring
the way gulls stare, faces that now trained their eyes
toward the black in their cups. We were warm there,
though all of us too poor to buy anything
much, and when our envy of the seeming feasts
enjoyed at neighboring tables overrode
the pleasure of a warm, dry seat, we walked back
into the cold. But outside, we found a city
transformed. The oppressive clouds were gone.
Bright sunlight filled the streets with a humid
warmth, and a bicyclist sped past, both wheels
spinning fountains. The crevasses between stones
still held the old rain, but the flat boardwalk
pavement dried rapidly as we found our way
back to the water. It danced playfully now,
splashing against the stone bulwark and topping
the rails, great blue arcs flashing and falling.
Where nothing but gray fury had been before,

not a calm green bay spread before us, and in the distance—
we could see it now—the Irish Sea. We stood
leaning against the iron rail, and I looked down
to the base of the wall, some ten feet, where the gray,
brief beach strand met the base of the boardwalk hill.
Two boys sat in the sand. They were laughing
like fools in a mess of green bottles, skinny arms
akimbo, so damn drunk at midday and soaking wet,
when one stood up to piss a puddle filled the hollow
where he'd sat. They were brimful of joy. No one else
saw them, and I didn't point them out. I envied them—
that wild pleasure, shameless abandon, the ease
with which they lay there on the edge of their country,
staring in the wind's cold mouth and laughing.

Ata Moharreri

Mailbox Blues

For Tennessee Saeed Moharreri

I know not every letter sent arrives.
Termites tunnel through soil.
A magnolia tree is to my right.

Night washes over my missing numbers.
I look into a leafless sky
at the bottom of a puddle inside a rut.

"Not all lucky stars get counted,"
the magnolia, stiff and twisted, reminds itself.
In the middle of faded verbena I stand,

my post covered with rime.
A shaving of light brushes against my door.
Mites chew secrets that haven't left the tree.

Three stars disappear, and a barn owl hops
along a downward reaching branch.
The owl slips on dark without making a sound.

I stand near the chewed-up tree
and chatter from the stars keeps the owl awake.
We still have prayers to receive in this world.

Charon's Song

You won't live as old as your teeth
or keys in your pocket.

No half dollars on your eyes
for a boat ride to the afterlife:
you won't live as old as your teeth.

You'll outlast rabbits and bees,
and a poodle will not outlive you.

You might outshine sons and ladies
but never the sun, seeing that
you won't live as old as your teeth,

though you could make it to eighty,
which is a long shot with a golden tail.

Rings stick around, rivers endure,
and what's unsaid becomes half spoken.
You won't live as old as your teeth.

D.E. St. John

Elevations II

The horses run unbridled across the plain.
My heart rivers cold blood. I think of how
a horse seen from the side and from the front

are the same, the way I am both in Italy,
burning silently, and also in the present day
in America, thinking of the past the way a cicada

never does, never would think about its shell,
even as it continues to cling to the side
of its molting tree as though it were alive.

The horse, the shells, and myself: we are all
machines operating in the light of seasons.
It was Spring then, and it is Spring now.

To tell the truth, I am afraid of blood.
the way it pools within the body, surging
into the brain without warning, without

giving us a chance to remember horses.

Elevations III

Soil speaks into the air: it says the sun
is a white dress. The air that swoops
through its sleeves is nothing like a song.

Soil speaks into the air and gives thanks
for the dead. Our steps are moments
of silence. If I listen, I can remember

the voices of the children outside the basilica,
kicking a ball against its wall, laughing,
each kick shaking the bones inside.

Trenna Sharpe

Constellation of Masquerades

Scientists have created Anteros out of a fruitfly.
A simple gene tweak and a bug becomes a god,
irresistible to every other fly that finds it now.
This means nothing for us, for the gods do not exist
outside the stairwells of imagination, the whirligig
nature of human desire. We're in love! we say.
We're in love! With the open palms of history,
with the potatoes growing silently in the garden.
I could grow moss in my pocket, and never be alone.
I am lost without it! I am not lost. I am standing at a threshold
of mossiness. There is cold weather coming in either direction.
The wind curls itself around my body and sings
and it tells me that every chemical in my body passed first
through the body of a star, so I have nothing to worry about.
I was dead before I reached me. My spindly legs are the result
of the atmosphere, the rough journey down to the face of this earth.
I'm a crippled constellation masquerading as human.
The glint in my eye is more than just an expression. My sense
of direction is skewed for good reason. I'll never find a point
            to end on.
Everything happens in circles. One day my life
will get caught in the orbit of another, and no one
will know which way to follow.

By the Lagan

Dear Stephen, I'm a sucker for uppers.
I like the way my heart drops.
If somebody punched me in the face
I would be stronger than I am now.
I'm younger than that now. I'm younger
than that now, the song says. Over and over
I try to say the night comes in a-falling
and the clouds whisper in its ear.
I put daffodils on my bedside table;
the sun sleeps next to me. I put
all my loves in each line. I don't
have many. I think in some other life
I could be in love with you.
Not this one. I like your heart, Stephen.
People don't say that enough.
Years ago it was night in my brain.
I want to take the sun and send it
somewhere you could find. Nobody
remembers what a sunset looks like,
Stephen. We have to keep waking,
speak to the foreign countries of each
morning when the light cuts to the quick.
If the sun ever finds you I hope
it was me that sent it. My shoes are coated
in dirt from so many cities. Sometimes
it gets so hot I can't feel where my body
ends and the air begins. Love
sometimes is like that. I tell
the heat my body loves it.

Daniel Myers

Landmarks

Alright, to make it back
                home, turn left at the oak tree,

right at the church shaped like a backwards L,
straight when passing the bank

which would be my cousin Jim if he were
a structural edifice. It's a big building.

                And as I am landmarking,
I know all will be lost—or more specifically me—

that I've as good a shot making it back home in a straight line
as a young family of ants traveling the Pacific Ocean

on a paper airplane. But I don't stop
running. I don't turn around. I love

the idea of occupying my nowhere
in the middle of someone else's somewhere.

My Jewish grandmother warned our family's curse is
                we love the things that destroy us. . ..

                after I told her the last
name of my German girlfriend.

I can't blame her. My grandfather quit drinking
                after he died of liver failure.

And the man she would've rather married
died alone in a trench during World War Two.

Only the most random landmarks ever stick:

127

strewn t-shirts, roadside funeral flowers,

waterfalls, Dr. Pepper cans. Bigfoot footprints.
My own. The time my brother hid my grandfather's

tie in the pig-shaped cookie jar. Or when the wind
unlatched the bird feeder and sent the cockatiel feed

spinning through our swing set like a dust devil.
How after dinner at a Mexican restaurant my mother

started sobbing but didn't know why. She didn't know why
her mother had *it*, she said. Her father had *it*

though he never admitted *it*. But she knew she had *it*
                    and prayed I did not have *it* too.

A tree is a questionable landmark, especially at night.
That is, unless someone carved a Santa Claus face

within its bark. If that's the case, I'm a mile from home.
                    The closer the more I understand

the quirks of every step, the exact way the sidewalk tugs
my calves, how each tree bends when the wind slips

its fingers through the branches, the everlasting
sprinklers and the corgis that dance beneath them.

My mom can differentiate
her children by the sound of our stair footsteps.

She compared my stair descent to a koala bear
who had just attended a lengthy tea party, soft

yet eager. Quick and purposeful.
At the end of a long run sometimes my brain blurs

like a television with a snapped antennae.
I'm so tired. Afraid my left leg might snap

after the next step. My head might fall off
and roll into my neighbor's rosegarden.

The sky might trip over a cloud and bleed
into my eyes. It's worst right after I finish.

If I don't collapse, I can't stop wheezing until
after I step in the shower and flip on the water.

Then I collapse. My grandmother was never
meant to be a mother. You didn't even have to

know her, my mother says, just look at her,
and you'd know, if you looked, really looked at her,

you couldn't miss the way she tucked in her emotions
like an oversized jersey. The way grief and crimson

lipstick shaped the edges of her jagged smile.
Always she knew exactly where she was.

My body seems more fossil than flesh
                    in that I cling to the places I have been,

my tennis shoe imprints more bone than my own.
So I run somewhere else and hope I am

too fatigued to notice the way my wry roads
intersect. I pray my sidewalks empty, my buildings

nondescript, my trees without inscriptions.
To become too lost and exhausted inside my own body

to recognize the landmarks that have stood longer
than I have: the streetlight beneath the North Star,

the spider webs which connect one monkey bar
to the next, and the shifting yet determined

        cadence of my family's footsteps.

Cody Taylor

Inner Dynamics

Everything sings here: The soft hum of
the woman speaking Portuguese behind me,
the train's own orchestra rumbling on the tracks
on the way from Cais do Sodré. I close my eyes and listen,
the world seems as soft as the vibrato of my mother's voice
the day her mother died. And then, the train's chatter
becomes the staccato rhythm of my childhood friends
stammering over each other as they learned to imitate
the language of our parents.

       I never really learned all that language.
I'm just piecing together meaning from momentary flashes,
like the faces looking out of the train speeding
in the opposite direction of mine. All of my love
is just an inarticulate murmur. I can't even say
I know you, because I lose focus. You get blurry.
The pitch of your being warbles and fades inside me
as the train you are on speeds farther from mine.

But I remember the timbre of your voice when we last spoke,

trembling and worrying and stumbling. I remember each syllable
like this sunset. Like the waves lapping against the beach.
Like the forests of home, like crickets chirping, the moonlight
on your face. Somehow, the earth's every note sounds like saying
"I'm sorry" to funeral guests you hardly know.

Like the orchestra inside this train carrying me home.
As we slow, the crescendo is happening. It's always happening;
it's waiting for us at the stop we're always leaving from.

Your Poetry Is Dying, So Here Is a Eulogy

The sun has set in Arizona, and the Hohokam's
art still lives on nearby rocks.
It's colder than we thought it could be.
The desert's shade isn't so much black
as blue. Its gravel and grit shift
beneath my feet. I can't stop
pacing towards the wild dark.

I know the path by the faulty saguaro.
I pick a few desert flowers while trekking
from our makeshift camp. At four stops,
I place bouquets of penance. I remember
the poetry you wrote for me. Soon the world

spirals into twisted history. I cut my hair.
I tear off my clothes. I lie down.

There are no homes left. But I watch
the river as it drifts by. It never dries.
And, in time, the saguaros all grow strong.

Halley Corapi

Something to Indicate That

This isn't about you, though I can see why
you'd think so, the two of us sitting side by side
in the car that flipped but barely made it through—
like your parents, whose inevitable separation
due to empty nest syndrome is the current topic
of your concern. You ask me to put your mind at ease
but I'm telling you now I don't have the proper training
or tools, and I prefer you alive and confused.

Confusion is what brought us here, I think,
and you're slipping off again, but I can't write a poem
for you so please don't take it personally.
When you feel sick, I'll research symptoms.

But we already know there's no medicine for the way
a man unfolds. You won't swallow it anyway
and so you lie, swear I'm worse for your health than I am
for my own, and I understand. It's all wrong, I know,
but I understand. You're not dying, you say.
I don't hurt you, you say. You just bruise easy, that's all.

I understand.

But this isn't about you, though I can see
why you'd think so, and I'm asking you to stop—
stop squalling, stop spitting, stop spilling your insides
all over the dashboard like a child with nothing to lose
but everything he doesn't have yet anyway,
while all the words I try to drag from my throat
still live alone in the places I don't go anymore.

The Sunlight Says to Childhood—

The birch trees peeling in the bitter light
know what no one could ever want from me.

A broken toy at the bottom of the lake
mumbles a jagged rhyme that counts the hours
backwards into light. If I skip a stone, the water
knows I'm fading. The loons at night cry out
to mourn the drowned. The moon upon the surface
is my face escaped from memory.

Some days my heart's a tree, a toy,
a tiny stone that skips three beats
and strains to hear the grief of birds
that know what dies, and what descends beside it.

Hudson Myracle

How to Love Your Inevitable Doom

Hold it the way your parents did
when they carried your sleeping,
4-year old body from the car to the bedroom.
Tuck its hair behind its ears;
look it in the eyes.
Stop paying attention to media
that tells you that your doom
is not beautiful enough for us.
Listen to a lot of NPR.
They know that my doom
is just as good as your doom.
Ask your doom about its childhood.
Ask it about your childhood.
Ask it about a childhood
that has never even happened.
Find out what it believes in,
and I mean really believes in.
Don't settle for one-word answers
—really dig in.
Don't be abrasive.
Kiss it slowly.
Let your doom come to you.

Love in the blast

We stood in front of a steam boat.
I had forgotten all the rivers I've lived near.

I almost wanted to exist in the past then.
For a second, I was daunted by the moment.

I wanted to pound on the glass
Surrounding my entire life.

You were on-looking with a broken heart,
The kind of break that will ache in bad weather.

Now I understand,
We found a hole in time to wedge our love into.

Your heart was heavy with funeral plans and
A time capsule you have suddenly stuffed with memories.

At any moment we experience annihilation.

I don't want to grow weak in the face of devastation.
Not anyone's, but yours in particular.

Every now and then I remember that we
Are responsible for the living world,
The small bird of community cradled in our palms.

In front of the mississippi river
I considered your anger, my anger
Your pain, my pain
And your love, my love.

Lacy Snapp

Becoming a Ghost

Ghosts sit around my dining room table without place
settings. They follow neighborhood children to the bus
stop. Pass me the shampoo in the shower. Join me for
my morning stretches, downward-facing dog, ghost garbs
fall, cover their heads, reveal transparency. Two bicker
in the backseat on my drive to work, to the grocery store.
One doodles in the freezer aisle, gets distracted fogging glass
with his breath, drawing smiley faces with his silky ghost
fingers. A shopper reaches through him to get a frozen
pizza, my ghost glares, refuses to dissipate. Lady ghost
sits beside me in bed, complains about my tableside lamp,
it keeps her up. I click it off, lay silent in the blackness, replay
those moments that have long passed, moments I didn't speak
loud enough. My ghosts and I wander in Willow Springs Park.
I lead the V of this flock of geese, their linen white limbs billow
in the wind, scraps left behind like feathers on the grass.
They squawk at passersby, people who don't look at me—
chase these strangers to their cars, nipping at their heels.
One ghost sheds her veil, puts it in the tub to soak overnight.
When she isn't looking, I slip beneath the water, try it on, relish
in the unseen, love how it feels to officially have no face or name.

Daily Routine

During the summers, I start pulling forgotten
      lumber from storage units every morning
            by eight a.m. The current stack—a mound
of beech bowed from years of neglect. *It's shit*
      wood anyways, my dad says, *splinters and cracks*
            no matter how carefully it's handled.
Twelve feet above my head, I try to figure how I will manage
      to get it down—climb on the lower rows, pray
            they hold my weight, where random boards
protrude like harpoons lost in Moby Dick's side.

While I ascend, simple phrases catch in my ears
      as spider webs do in my hair and branch out—
            spread, link together as I take little pieces
from radio commercials or mainstream song lyrics
      that I wish I didn't know the words to. The first
            half of the workday is a time for repeating:
Step up. Balance. Pull the highest board out. Let it tip
      to the ground. Step off. Pick up. Carry
            to its new home. Double check that its
aligned. Return to the stack—As my body shifts

into automation, my mind tests its ability to withstand
      the pressure of memory. A poem begins
            as the morning dew evaporates, starts with
an image gathered unexpectedly: the perfectly preserved
      mouse carcass in a gap between two rows. Silverfish
            slipping into their own reclaimed utopias.
Carpenter bees flirting with overhead beams—while they
      tunnel, sawdust falls, sticking to the cobwebs
            I already wear, pairing together
borrowed lyrics with beings that merely needed a voice.

Repeat until lunchtime, stomach growling and stanza
       about to burst from my mouth, I scavenge
              for a discarded block in the scrap box, settle
for a two-by-four wedge. The poem pours out
       as my sandwich goes in, taking time between
              each bite to tap the cadence on my work
bench stool. For all the hours past noon, the stacking-
       lumber-process resumes while my brain
              takes time to decompress. Pencil and cubed
poem in my pocket, I wait for the final words to find me
       —unmistakable as a newly forged splinter
beneath the skin.

Honeymoon

Foxes go out with frost tipping on their boots. To ransack
sleeping dens and leave their tracks not hither
      nor yon on the slopes
of the blue hill. Fieldstones wait out in the empty field. To be
harvested. And the hearts of the dead are turning ripe again.
Shouldering up dirt as tuber. And radish. A spade

watches the night go by standing on its head. All moony. But back
inside the wine pulls no tricks. It's our bones that take turns at
fouling up Jacob's Ladder. We make faces at the dark. We screw
our brains out and then lie there and listen. Windchimes.
Seaming the night back together. Like lead veins in
      a stained-glass window.

Monofilament

Somebody put something archaic in my denominator.
Winsome as a winsome drapery. Busted as a leather shoe

dipped in bronze. Turns out funny in the end that
all Booth really wanted was to make a birdhouse out of Old Abe's

transatlantic prow. Having as he had then more birds
than boxes to put them in. Nobody buries their secret treasures

in their own backyard. That was the easy part. Inevitably so.
That was the part covered in deadly ribbons and bows.

Olivia Townsend

Stag

I
My roommates and I watch a movie
About the depths of human consciousness
And how this relates to dinosaurs.
I am fascinated by the body's resilience,
The many wounds a body can endure before
Licking itself to death. Pain
Hovers around the room like a bored
Balloon, quiet enough it could be mine
As if my pain could fit inside a balloon.
I don't like movies I can relate to because
I relate too much to sin and thinness
Of emotion. There are so many ways to die
And I am in the middle of so many.
My roommates are sleeping.
My mouth-hole is a guest
In their dreams.

II
We are in the movie theatre
But we are also in the movie
And there is no way out of either
Like the drive to death
Or attempting to explain a theory
Without logic or ideology.
None are possible, like seeing all sides
Of a sphere. Though we can try
With a little help from some white light
And mirrors, reflect what is not
Onto what is. Everyone
Is a zombie in this movie.
Too bad that's been done before.
Too bad the blood does not look more
Real to me, then perhaps I might feel
More squeamish about my own
Existence. Perhaps then
You might like me.

Shrine

I see a dead dog in the road.
It has holes in it shaped like hearts
which burn when I look through them.

This is a feeling I know well.
If I had a moment, I would watch it rise.

Decomposition is incorrectly described
as a "process," as if a course
to resolution.

Slow in its straining to a near-off something better.
Evolving to becoming both and other than itself.
A new whole self.

Yet I can't, in the thick of watching
think of this gorgeous body deteriorating
as a consequence of dying,
or of having even existed at all
as, however small, a resolution for
the one who just did the dying.
Tell me, do you want it?

Jared Steiman

No Rack

After Metka Krašovec

Is it so easy to break

skin? I have grown brittle in soul, torn in
heart, already—but this body was sculpted
and fired

in the blistering center of a storm cloud.

It fell to the earth and left a crater where it
struck. While I have lain sorrowfully inside, it has
climbed mountains

to piss in the purest snow rivers,

crossed an ocean to stand on the graves of kings.
The blood it has tasted has nourished me, and
I have tried

to weep through its impenetrable eyes.

300 Dead Catfish, or: At the River's Edge with a Box of My Father's Ashes

which I set on a kind, flat stone while
I remove my shirt,
and fold it, and lay it in the
grass, and unlace my boots (his
boots) and place them in the grass,
and my socks, my pants,
folded,
in the grass, at the water's edge
I step out of my plaid boxers and my full
body shines under the sun and I fold them,
too, and lay them in the grass,
lift the lid from that little wood box, scoop
a teaspoon of my father
with three hooked fingers
and bring him to my lips
and spread him across my cheeks
and press him into my brow
and beneath my jaw
and when I lean out over this water, find,
in our reflection, that yes
I am wearing my father's face
on my face,
hooked fingers scoop more
massage what is left of us into each
of the soft inside of my elbows,
behind my knees and between my legs
and up the length of my spine
and between every toe
and when my full body shines under him
we fold and lay in the grass.

When I finish crying, I lean out
over this water and find—

except for the radiant streaks beneath each eye—
my father regarding himself
for the last time
and he walks us into the water.

Elizabeth Rose Bruce

The Poet at Sunset

Again you've found yourself in that brief and
translucent moment, before darkness displaces
the sun, that moment with which the poet is destined
to waste their life, carving colors into language
like termites eating constellations into a rotten
wooden door to nowhere. Isn't that the poem? That
entrance into the same place you've exited, shrouded
by the moment before shadow overcomes light.

Refuge

The sparrow builds her nest wherever she may like,
in some odd tree or windowsill, god forbid the gutter.
She collects the scraps of others, loved ones and
strangers, braids them with feathers and weeds.

Last week, I saw her little wreath on the sidewalk,
intentional and complicated enough, even in its disarray,
to have been made for some small family. The mocking-
bird song began just as twilight fell over her wreckage.

At home I locked my door and I wondered what great
storm tossed the nest from its corner, there on the sidewalk,
for any passerby to stop and rummage as they please.
A friend tells me that her species is invasive, threatening.

I too might have walked through that very same storm
to get home, mourned my feathers and twigs with fury
if the rain had come screaming and firing at the windows,
and all that anyone had to say was that I didn't belong.

Cas McKinney

Pelican Thoughts / Cinnamon Beach, FL

The pelicans hover in ritual
fluid bodies above waves with
old wings extending,
shadowing new
They summon wind &
learn to harvest a fresh breeze

These things sustain them
as well as they sustain me
we are hungry and content.
They pray before a meal &

I hear my mother in the echo
of squawking amens
I wonder if we picture God the same way
My mother myself and the birds
is he always a flash of feathers and flesh

descending into the crest of a wave?
their religion will always be a mystery
I am a still observer a guest at the table
to an unforeseen feast. Bodies in the water.
a witness to slaughter.

From my beach chair
I watch a spray of silver
fish scatter,
survivors envisioning a wrath of feathers.
triumphant squawks after some slither
into a maw - from the sound
perhaps a first kill.

The flesh is taken
& received.
The day is bright
above rejoicing wings.

Visiting Home / Anticipatory Grief

I want to lay on my parent's bed with the ease of the snooze button,
I want it to be a habit, like coming home
to see them aging.
mostly I want to forget about that.

At home it is easy, a habit of pretending
in everything we see. Our pictures hang over us
and there are no gray hairs, no crow's feet.
Here I see myself, never older than 8 &
I like the way I am fashioned
into an uncomplicated thing.
I try to become her for awhile

When I say go to say goodnight, I'm eye-level
with the doorknob. I look at it and the paint has never chipped
under decades of hands. My fist is small,
and I hear a child's knock in the light echoing,
something ashamed, afraid of the quiet
and the hinge that will always creak.
The lights are on, the bed is turned down,
and they appear somewhere in all the years they've known me—

I'm never sure how old my parents are in the present
or memory. My mother wears a t-shirt
from my middle school,
my father's is older than me. Timeless
comfort. He wore it the night I woke
the house up screaming. I was 6 &
somewhere in a dream I discovered mortality.
I understood the years between us
as they opened my bedroom door
and asked what the hell was wrong with me.
They listened & I explained what they knew:
death comes for all things.

They carried me to their room,
comforting me with abstracts like heaven and Jesus
between shushing yawns.
We settled in, and my father snored a lullaby
stretching like a white noise machine—
the same one whistling now.
My mother basks in lamplight rereading a Bible.
I sit on the edge of a bed made for two adults
and the alarm goes off. I'm grown,
it's time to say goodnight.

I don't pray, but I tell God what I want:
I want to fit between them one more time,
please,
I want to stay the night.

Jude Keef

Thoughts in the Presence of an Old Stranger

He walks up to me as I'm walking back to my car,
and I say hi, because hi is what you say when
you don't remember a name. His name
silent in the mind
Like a well-timed change in the seasons.
It is not a well-timed change
in the seasons. False fall.
The leaves stay green and stapled
to the trees, the sky still bright, but
the wind grips the bare arms,
hairs rising, protesting, shouting
who remembered to think about me?
To care for me
and to keep me warm. To remind me
to dig out the sweaters in my closet.
Right beside the box I was supposed
to be reminded not to dig out.
It's a simple box, really.
Old junks and papers, receipts that no one would
care about, maybe some flower clippings, and at the bottom
a folded sweater that belonged to someone else—
a sweater which stays on the mind,
when I should be thinking about clothes, not people
when I'm supposed to be thinking about names
or weather or about
how I really shouldn't have stopped—
I should've just waved and kept walking.
I have to go to home, or I have to go get lunch—
no I have plans for lunch, sorry,
or I can't sit and talk, I gotta prepare for a meeting too,
because lunch is just time I should be working,
feeding mind as body,
mens sana in corpore sano.
Just like the Romans believed. When it was after lunch

and they all went to the baths, which
was about bathing, sure, but it was really about
everything else, about working out in the gym, or
about reading in the library
in the baths, or about trying to secure
a dinner invite from a noble. Everyone bathes, and
everyone eats. The present is never just the present.
It's a moment that draws past to present, present to future.
No one stops for a moment to just rest!
I'm still standing before the man,
staring, waiting for a sign from God. Maybe a sign
that I can't know everything, or maybe
that I should stop and listen for a moment. When
he says Whelp, I'm gonna go work
on that thing due
tomorrow, and the belts of the mind slacken
no more gears to turn or pistons to fire.

No One Laughs

The leaves stumble and turn. It is autumn
and they fall, but not because they know it.

A person walks up a hill, and feels the sun
soak into their black tee as they both crest.

The sun does not cut into chill; Open, uncovered
arms of trees match those of the flesh walking below.

The coats line hooks neatly and accent chair backs
where they were plucked before their time.

A person walks in a knit cardigan and sweats
through her shirt. Her skirt catches no breeze.

Friends discuss weather and winter parties. One
suggests swimming on his birthday, and no one laughs.

The leaves stumble and trip. It is still autumn,
and they still fall, but not because they want to.

Contributor Biographies

Liz Albert received a BA in Humanities from UTC, an MA from the Johns Hopkins University's Writing Seminars and an MA in English (Rhetoric and Composition) from the University of Maryland College Park. A six-week gig teaching writing to academically advanced teens in 1984 led to Liz's 30+ year career at the Johns Hopkins Center for Talented Youth.

Bridgette Bates' debut collection *What Is Not Missing Is Light* was the recipient of Rescue Press' Black Box Poetry Prize. Her work has appeared in *Boston Review*, *Fence*, *jubilat*, *PEN Poetry Series*, and *Kirkus Reviews*. She lives in Los Angeles.

Julia Beach lives in Rhode Island where she works as a graphic designer, content writer/editor, and woodturner. Her poems have appeared in *Hayden's Ferry Review*, *Occulum*, *Barren Magazine*, and *Hobo Camp Review*.

Mark Bilbrey (1979-2018) was a lifelong poet and lover of literature and language. His poems have been published in *Versal*, *ACTION YES*, *42 Opus*, *LIT*, *Ghost House*, and *Straylight*. He developed a keen interest in fine cheeses and became an outstanding cheese monger after leaving academia. He was also an enthusiastic birder. Mark was a quiet soul, a loving son, a patient brother, a silly uncle, a quick and lasting friend, and a smiling face with a great laugh for everyone who crossed his path.

David Breitkopf attended UTC from 1979-1983. After school, David continued to write poetry, started writing fiction, some of which has been published over the years. He was also a reporter and editor for various daily newspapers. Today he teaches English Language Arts (ELA) in New York City.

Jennifer Brown (she/her) lives with her partner and a funny-looking dog in Montpelier, Vermont, on unceded Abenaki land. Formerly a teacher, currently a part-time manager at a grocery co-op, she dabbles in bookbinding, sewing, baking, birdwatching, drawing, painting, knitting, and gardening, in addition to writing poetry and nonfiction. She got started writing poetry in Rick Jackson's poetry workshops and UHON 101 at UTC between 1988 and 1992, and went on to study poetry and CNF at the University of Maryland and the University of Houston with folks like Stanley Plumly, Phillis Levin, Edward Hirsch, and Mark Doty, all of whom she met during Meacham Writers' Workshops. Her work has appeared in *Copper Nickel*, *Orison Anthology*, *Cimarron Review*, *Zone 3*, *Twyckenham Notes*, and *Cincinnati Review*. Her first poetry collection, *Natural Violence*, was published in 2022 by Brick Road Poetry Press.

Elizabeth Rose Bruce is a poet and creative nonfiction writer from Chattanooga, Tennessee. Liz has previously been published in *Arkana*, *Susurrus*, *The Sequoya Review*, and *Global Poemic*. She is currently an MFA candidate at The University of North Carolina Greensboro where she is Poetry Editor of *The Greensboro Review*.

Halley Corapi is the Programs & Marketing Manager for The Porch Writers Collective, a literary nonprofit based in Nashville, Tennessee. She serves as a reader for The Porch's print literary magazine *SWING*. She has also done copywriting and production work in the political messaging sphere, working for Democrats, Independents, and advocacy groups around the country.

Rachel Landrum Crumble recently retired from teaching high school, having previously taught kindergarten through college. She has published in *The Porterhouse Review*, *Typishly*, *SheilaNaGig*, *Common Ground Review*, *Spoon River Review*, *The Banyan Review* and others. Her first poetry collection, *Sister Sorrow*, was published by Finishing Line Press in January 2022. She lives with her husband of forty-three years, a jazz drummer, and near two of their three adult children, and two adorable grand twins. poetteachermom.com is her website.

Greg Delisle lives in Ithaca, New York, with his wife Anu Rangarajan. His writing has appeared in several print and multimedia journals, and once on NPR's *All Things Considered*.

Keith Driver was born in Massachusetts. He lives in Charlottesville, Virginia. His poems have appeared in *jubilat*, *Bridge*, *Third Bed*, *B O D Y*, and elsewhere.

Will Flowers lives in the Colorado Front Range region and works in both digital- and built-environment accessibility for people with disabilities. His poetry has been included in various anthologies, including two editions of the *Southern Poetry Anthology*, as well as journals such as *Great River Review, Hunger Mountain,* and *Bellingham Review.* While he may be one of the only ADA Coordinators with an MFA in Creative Writing, when asked, he credits his time in Dr. Richard Jackson's poetry program with fomenting in him a lifelong personal and professional passion for civil rights and human dignity.

David Franke attended the Syracuse University graduate program in poetry and stayed at SU for a doctorate in Comp/Rhet. He has lately been focused on creative nonfiction and is finishing a memoir based in Iowa and Tennessee, and has started work on a "deep map" of the area around where he lives, the Tully Valley in Onondaga County, New York, a site of great violence against the environment: his SU teacher Hayden Carruth called nearby Onondaga Lake "The oldest killed lake in America." Here, in this despite-it-all beautiful Finger Lakes region, he has worked at a nearby state college for about twenty-five years and raised four boys. He is very grateful to have been part of the undergraduate program at UTC.

Hunter Grey received his MFA at the University of North Carolina Wilmington, where he also served as poetry editor for *Ecotone* magazine. He is currently pursuing his MTS at Boston University. His work has previously appeared in *Pigeon Pages* and *The Heart's Many Doors.*

Paul Guest is the author of four collections of poetry, most recently *Because Everything Is Terrible*, and a memoir, *One More Theory About Happiness.* His writing has appeared in *Poetry, The Paris Review, Tin House, Slate, New England Review, The Southern Review, The Kenyon Review, Ploughshares,* and numerous other publications. A Guggenheim Fellow and Whiting Award winner, he lives in Charlottesville, Virginia.

Danielle Hanson is author of *The Night Is What It Eats*, winner of the Elixir Press Prize (forthcoming), *Fraying Edge of Sky*, winner of the Codhill Press Poetry Prize, and *Ambushing Water*, finalist for the Georgia Author of the Year Award, and editor of a book of literary criticism and this book. Her poetry was the basis for a puppet show at the Center for Puppetry Arts. Previously, she has been Artist-in-Residence at Arts

Beacon and Writer-in-Residence for Georgia Writers. She is Marketing Director for Sundress Publications and the inaugural Poet Laureate of Costa Mesa, California. She teaches poetry at UC Irvine.

Magdelyn Hammond Helwig is the Writing Programs Director at Furman University. She specializes in verbal-visual collaboration, visual rhetoric, and multimodal composition. Her work can be found in *The Ekphrastic Review* (2016), *The Walt Whitman Quarterly Review* (2016), *Plainsongs* (2017), and *Women's Ways of Making* (2020, Utah State University Press).

Laura E. Howard, a UTC and Indiana University graduate, teaches English at Baylor School. Her poems have appeared in *Complete Idiot's Guide to Writing Poetry* and *Third Coast*, and her awards include First Prize, Academy of American Poets University Prize, Indiana University, 1999.

Born in Chattanooga, Tennessee, in 1971, **Ted E. Howard (1971-2015)** was a violinist, poet, computer programmer, and gardener. He was a Brock Scholar at UTC and completed his MFA in Poetry at the University of Maryland. He found peace in his garden where he and his wife created a wildlife habitat with their rescue cats. He passed away in 2015 after a short battle with cancer.

Melanie Jordan is a Tennessee writer who currently lives in Newnan, Georgia. Her book, *Hallelujah for the Ghosties*, was published by Sundress Publications. Her work has appeared or is forthcoming in *Iowa Review, Birminghman Poetry Review, EuropeNow, Poetry Southeast*, and others.

Jude Keef is a writing consultant for the University of Tennessee at Chattanooga and a recent graduate in creative writing and classics. Their work focuses on the intersection between identity and the past, and can be found in the *Sequoya Review* and the *Southern Literary Festival Anthology*.

Helga Kidder lives in the Tennessee hills. She is a graduate of UTC and Vermont College. Her poems have recently been published in *Orbis, Conestoga Zen*, and *Tipton Poetry Journal*. She has five collections of poetry, *Wild Plums, Luckier than the Stars, Blackberry Winter,*

Loving the Dead, which won the Blue Light Press Book Award 2020, and *Learning Curve*—poems about immigration and assimilation.

Caroline Klocksiem holds a BA in Humanities from The University of Tennessee at Chattanooga (2001) and an MFA in Creative Writing from Arizona State University. After decades of teaching college-level English, she is currently pursuing her Masters in Social Work to support the empowerment of marginalized people through anti-oppressive and identity-affirming therapy practice. Originally from South Carolina, she lives with her family in Las Cruces, New Mexico on land of the Manso and Piro-Manso-Tiwa people and in the valley of the Organ Mountains-Desert Peaks National Monument. She holds endless gratitude and love for Mark Bilbrey (UTC class of 2000), to whom this and every poem is dedicated.

Jami Loree lives in Oviedo, Florida, where she works as a technical writer. She earned a Master's degree in Creative Writing from the University of Washington.

Taylor Loy has published poetry in *Poet Lore*, *Marlboro Review*, *Redivider*, *RHINO*, and other journals. He is a two-time Fulbright grant finalist for a poetry project in Slovenia. In 2024, he completed a PhD in Science & Tech Studies at Virginia Tech and lives with his partner, Rebecca Shelton, and son near Nashville, Tennessee.

Liz Marlow is a Jewish American writer. She is the author of *They Become Stars* (Slapering Hol Press 2020). Her work has been included in Best Small Fictions and nominated for the Pushcart Prize, Best of the Net, Best Microfiction, and Best New Poets anthologies. Additionally, her work has appeared or is forthcoming in *Beloit Poetry Journal*, *The Greensboro Review*, *The Idaho Review*, *The Minnesota Review*, *Valparaiso Poetry Review*, and elsewhere. She is Editor-in-Chief of *Minyan Magazine* and a coeditor of Slapering Hol Press. She earned her MFA in creative writing from Western Michigan University.

Khaled Mattawa is the William Wilhartz Professor of English Language and Literature at the University of Michigan. His latest book of poems is *Fugitive Atlas* (Graywolf, 2020). A MacArthur Fellow, he is the current editor of *Michigan Quarterly Review* and has received a National Endowment for the Arts Translation

Fellowship, the Alfred Hodder Fellowship from Princeton University, a Guggenheim Fellowship, an Academy of American Poets award, and has twice won the PEN Award for Poetry in Translation.

Kristi Maxwell is the author of eight books of poems, including *Goners*, winner of the Wishing Jewel Prize; *Realm Sixty-Four*, editor's choice for the Sawtooth Poetry Prize and finalist for the National Poetry Series; and *Hush Sessions*, editor's choice for the Saturnalia Books Poetry Prize. She's an associate professor of English at the University of Louisville.

L.S. McKee is the author of *Creature, Wing, Heart, Machine* from Zone 3 Press. She holds a BA from the University of Tennessee at Chattanooga and an MFA from the University of Maryland. She was a Wallace Stegner Fellow in poetry at Stanford and has taught writing at several universities, including MIT. Currently, she is Coordinator of Writing Across the Curriculum at the University of Georgia and lives in Athens, Georgia, with her family.

Cas McKinney (she/her) is a poet from Cleveland, Tennessee. She graduated from the University of Tennessee at Chattanooga with a BA in English: Creative Writing. Cas continues to write and study as an MFA candidate at Georgia College and State University. Her writing focuses on family, religion, and time.

Joshua Mensch is the author of *Because: A Lyric Memoir* (W. W. Norton), and the translator of two volumes of Czech poetry. He lives in the Czech Republic, where he edits the literary journal *B O D Y*.

Ata Moharreri has taught college courses in Massachusetts, California, and New York. He has an MFA from the University of Massachusetts Amherst.

Kelly Moore's nonfiction and poetry are published in *Mid-American Review*, *American Letters and Commentary*, *Bennington Review*, and *The Chattahoochie Review*, among other publications. She is currently a writing lecturer at the University of Houston, and in her free time she plays traditional and original songs around town with her banjo.

Rachel Morgan is the author of the chapbook, *Honey & Blood, Blood & Honey* (Final Thursday Press, 2017), and her work appears in the anthology *Fracture: Essays, Poems, and Stories on Fracking in America* (Ice Cube Press, 2017) and in *Prairie Schooner, Salt Hill, Boulevard, Mid-American Review, Barrow Street*, and elsewhere. She was the winner of the 2021 Fineline contest, and is a graduate of the Iowa Writers' Workshop. Currently she teaches at the University of Northern Iowa and is Poetry Editor for the *North American Review*.

Daniel Myers completed his MFA in the creative writing program at the University of Alabama. His work appears in *Blue Earth Review, DIAGRAM*, and *Puerto Del Sol*, among others. He attended the University of Tennessee from 2009 to 2013.

Hudson Myracle is a poet and essayist, farmer, cook, and fixer-upper in East Tennessee. They have published work in *The Bitter Southerner, Sobotka Magazine*, Ghost City Press, and elsewhere.

Terry Olsen practices Immigration & Nationality Law, and International Law. He is also currently the PDSO, and RO for Meharry Medical College. He is former Chair of the Tax Law Section of the Tennessee Bar Association, and is former Chair of the Immigration Law Section of the Tennessee Bar Association—having served as Chair of the TBA's Immigration Law Section for approximately eight terms since 2009, and has served twice as Chair of the International Law Section of the Tennessee Bar Association. He has given seminars at the following universities: University of Tennessee at Chattanooga, University of Tennessee at Knoxville, Southern Adventist University, Bryan College, Dalton State College, Oakwood University, the University of Alabama at Huntsville, Sewanee: The University of the South, National Taiwan University, and National Chung Hsing University. Terry is an alumnus of William and Mary Law School, Southern Illinois University, and the University of Tennessee at Chattanooga.

Karri Paul is a visual artist and poet living in Los Angeles with her husband Bradley, son Stellan, and dog Ducky. She is forever indebted to Rick's teaching about the creative process, close reading, political responsibility, and what it means to "travel beyond."

Bradley Paul is the author of three books of poetry. His work has appeared in *American Poetry Review, Boston Review, Fence*, and numerous other journals. A native of Baltimore, and a graduate of UTC and the Iowa

Writers' Workshop, he lives in Los Angeles with his wife Karri, whom he met in Rick's workshop. He writes for television.

Victoria Raschke is the author of *The Voices of the Dead* contemporary fantasy series and *Verona Green: a story of art & magic*. She and her partner co-own 1000Volt Productions which includes 1000Volt Press and the *WitchLit* podcast, hosted by Victoria. She has an MA in English from the University of Tennessee and lives in San Jose, California.

Teresa (Tree) Rogerson is an ecological landscape designer and massage therapist now that she is no longer (or more seldom is) a paddling instructor or camp counselor. She is single as of 2023 and doesn't expect that to change unless a very tall man wins her with kindness and beauty.

Jenny Sadre-Orafai is the author of *Dear Outsiders*, *Malak*, and *Paper Cotton Leather* and the co-author of *Book of Levitations*. She co-founded and co-edits *Josephine Quarterly* and teaches and mentors creative writers at Kennesaw State University and as part of the Periplus Collective.

Ever Saskya is from Hixson, Tennessee. She has a Ph.D. in Creative Writing from the University of Denver and an MFA in Creative Writing from Western Michigan University. She writes poetry, muti-genre stories, and created an art form to write and paint with sound waves. Although allergic, she completely loves dogs.

Charlie Scott grew up in Fort Payne, Alabama, and studied drama, poetry, and creative writing at the University of Tennessee, the University of Iowa, and the University of Houston. His poems have appeared in numerous magazines, anthologies, and journals, including *The New Republic*, *The Antioch Review*, *Gulf Coast*, *Zocalo Public Square*, *The Poetry Miscellany*, *Western Humanities Review*, *Intellectual Refuge*, *Mutabilis*, *The Sequoyah Review*, and *Alabama Poets: An Anthology* (Livingston University Press). He lives in Houston and is a founding member of Infernal Bridegroom Productions and the Catastrophic Theatre, the city's leading avant-garde theatre company for the past thirty years.

Richard Seehuus is Professor of English at Heartland Community College, where he has taught rhetoric and creative writing for twenty-two years.

Trenna Sharpe is from South Pittsburg, Tennessee. She has an MFA from the Program for Poets and Writers at UMass Amherst. Her recent poems can be found in *New England Review*, *North American Review*, *Sinister Wisdom*, *The Lifeboat*, and others. She lives and works in London, England.

Shannon Smith-Lee is Professor of English at Owens Community College in Toledo. He is a 1989 UTC graduate and a 1991 graduate of the Iowa Writer's Workshop. His poems have appeared in *Poetry*, *North American Review*, *Flyway*, *Stand*, and elsewhere. He is proud father to Emma, Isabel and Molly, and proud husband to Wade.

Lacy Snapp is a teacher and woodworker in East Tennessee. Her first chapbook, *Shadows on Wood* (Finishing Line Press), came out in 2021. She graduated with her MFA from Vermont College of Fine Arts in 2023 and her MA in English from East Tennessee State University in 2019.

Laurel Snyder is the author of several collections of poetry and many books for children, including *Orphan Island*, which was longlisted for the National Book Award, and *Charlie and Mouse*, which was awarded the Theodore Seuss Geisel Award in 2018. She teaches at Hamline University and lives in Atlanta.

D.E. (David) St. John currently teaches classes in Asian American and World literature at the University of Alabama in Huntsville. His poetry has previously appeared in *Prairie Schooner*, *Atlanta Review*, *B O D Y*, *Cutthroat: A Journal of the Arts*, *Cobalt*, and *Hunger Mountain*. He studied with Richard Jackson from 2003-2006.

Jared Steiman spends a lot of time thinking about his hands. This is the most important thing those hands have ever written:

> I plant a piece of my
> father in the ground, and
> become fragile. I shatter
> myself against the window,
> craning to see what flower
> will grow.

Cody Taylor is a writer from Tennessee. He completed his bachelor's degree at UTC's undergraduate creative writing program, and he currently resides in Chattanooga working with software. He hopes you're well.

TC Tolbert (he/him/hey grrrl) is a trans and genderqueer monkey-goat who lives in Tucson, Arizona, where s/he is the current Poet Laureate. Publications include *Gephyromania* (Ahsahta Press, 2014/Nightboat Books, 2022) and five chapbooks, including *The Quiet Practices*, winner of the 2023 Chad Walsh Chapbook Prize at *Beloit Poetry Journal*. TC is co-editor of *Troubling the Line: Trans and Genderqueer Poetry and Poetics* (Nightboat Books 2013).

Olivia Townsend lives, works, and wanders through Alabama with her partner, Trey, and their three cats, Odessa, CiCi, and Cher.

Laurie Perry Vaughen is a native of Tennessee and currently lives in Boston. Her poems have been recognized with awards from *Lullwater Review*, *Kalliope: A Journal of Women's Poetry*, *The Greensboro Review*, and the Ruminate Broadside Poetry Prize as a finalist for her poem "Billie Holiday on the Radio." She has performed with an Atlanta-based jazz trio, Three-Way Mirror, at Georgia Center for the Book in Atlanta, and Word of South Festival in Tallahassee. She is a recent graduate of the Sewanee School of Letters MFA program at the University of the South.

Catherine Wagner is author of five books of poems, including *Of Course* (Fence, 2020) and *Nervous Device* (City Lights, 2012). She co-edited *Contesting Extinctions: Decolonial and Regenerative Futures* (Lexington, 2021), a collection of environmental humanities essays. She recently helped to lead a successful unionization drive at Miami University, where she is professor of English. She lives in Cincinnati.

Sarah Wagner is a sculptor, installation artist, and writer whose work renders the frailties and strengths wrought by the dynamism of invisible forces onto worlds. Her sculptural installations often whisper questions about complex issues through ephemeral-looking animals made of sewn fabric over wood or steel armatures. A new author, she recently completed a memoir with drawings. Her art has been featured nationally and internationally in solo and group exhibitions including Projekt 0047 and Homie (Berlin), Muskegon Museum of Art, and Museum of Craft and Folk Art. She received a Pollock/Krasner Grant (2009) and a Joan Mitchell Fellowship (2014). She currently lives in Chattanooga, Tennessee. BFA, University of Tennessee at Chattanooga; Skowhegan School of Painting and Sculpture; MFA, California College of the Arts.

Acknowledgments

Liz Albert, "Nothing You Can See" from *Nothing You Can See* (Galvin Press, 1983).

Bridgette Bates, "A statue, an inescapable she" from *Boston Review*. "It is summer" from *FENCE*.

Julia Beach, "Danzig 1661," "In The Garden of Dread Reply" from *Cabinet of Heed*.

Jenn Brown, "Used" (as "Consignment") from *Phoebe and Natural Violence*, 2022, Brick Road Poetry Press. "Portrait of a Childhood with Abstract Art" from *NiftyLit*.

Paul Guest, "All I Know" from *American Poetry Review*.

Magdelyn Hammond Helwig, "Artemesia Gentileschi Painting Judith" from *The Ekphrastic Review*.

Danielle Hanson, "Domestic Troubles" from *diode poetry journal*. "Night's View of Fog" from *Aquila Review*.

Laura Howard, "Tiny Glasses Full of Gin" from *Third Coast*.

Melanie Jordan, "Charlie Brown in the Dead of Night" from *The Iowa Review* 33(1), 107–108. "The Kiss of the Cage" from *Birmingham Poetry Review*, Spring 2013, Volume 40.

Helga Kidder, "At St Mary's Convent" from *Poetry South* and in the book *Loving the Dead*. "Luna Moth" from *Conestoga Zen* and in the book *Learning Curve*.

Rachel Landrum Crumble, "Again" from *Sister Sorrow*, Finishing Line Press, 2022, and "Courage for a Year," in *Sheila-Na-Gig*, April 2019.

Jami Loree, "Some Regrets of My Own" from *PoetryMagazine.com*

Taylor Loy, "Work" from *Poet Lore*. "Construction Site, an approach to therapy" from *Marlboro Review*.

Liz Marlow, "Sara's Uniform" from *Small Orange*. "Avraham on Freedom" from *Superstition Review*.

Khaled Mattawa, "Double Portrait with Trains" from *Ismailia Eclipse*, Sheep Meadow Press, 1995. "Ecclesiastes" from *Tocqueville*, New Issues Press, 2010. "Beatitudes" from *Fugitive Atlas*, Graywolf Press, 2020.

Kristi Maxwell, "from SCROLL" from *Juked*. "Koala" from *La Vague Journal* and the book *Goners*, Green Linden Press, 2023.

L.S. McKee, "Alva and the Magnetic Resonance" from *Michigan Quarterly Review*. "Alva on Getting Dumped in the Desert" from *New Madrid*. Both poems from *Creature, Wing, Heart, Machine*, Zone 3 Press, 2023.

Joshua Mensch, "Prince Edward Island" from *Air/Light*, Issue 2, Winter 2021.

Ata Moharreri, "Mailbox Blues" from *Plume 10*. "Charon's Song" from *Gulf Coast*.

Kelly Moore, "The End of the Aquatic Apes" from *The Columbia Review*. "An Alternate Ending . . ." from *Mid-American Review*.

Rachel Morgan, "Child-Sized Pastoral" from *CutBank*, "These Mountains" from the anthology *Let Me Say This: A Dolly Parton Anthology*, Madville Publishing LLC, 2023.

Daniel Myers, "Landmarks" from *Puerto del Sol*.

Terry Olsen, three poems from *Pennsylvania English*, Fall '98, one poem from *Flint Hills Review*, Spring '99.

Bradley Paul, "Anyone Can Write a Poem" from *Pleiades*.

Victoria Raschke, "The Seventh Day" from *Pudding Magazine—The International Journal of Applied Poetry*.

Jenny Sadre-Orafai, "Testing a Pattern" and "Swim, Swam, Swum" from *New Orleans Review*.

Ever Saskya, "Opening the Mouths of Trees" from *The Porch Is a Journey Different from the House*, New Issues Press.

Charlie Scott, "1969" from *The New Republic*. "Paul Said This" from *Gulf Coast*.

Trenna Sharpe, "Constellation of Masquerades" from *The Sequoya Review*. "By the Lagan" from *The North American Review*.

Lacy Snapp, "Becoming a Ghost" from *Shadows on Wood*. "Daily Routine" from *Shadows on Wood: Women Speak*, Vol. 7.

TC Tolbert, "A man's arm may trick" commissioned for *New Voices: Contemporary Writers Confronting the Holocaust*; "Imago Dei" a ghazal written while looking at Roy McMakin's *Two Chests: One with No Knobs, One with Slightly Oversized Drawers*, commissioned by Tang Museum for *Energy In All Directions*, 2020, published in *Ninth Letter*, Winter 2021, and *The Quiet Practices*, Beloit Poetry Journal chapbook, 2023.

Catherine Wagner, both from *Of Course*, Fence 2020.

www.ingramcontent.com/pod-product-compliance
Lightning Source LLC
Chambersburg PA
CBHW021402090426
42742CB00009B/961